RICHARD J. DESOTO

AND

LIONEL C. BASCOM

To Antonia, Michele and Christina.

To Luci, Ginger and my daughters.

Excerpt from
"You Can't Go Home Again"
by Thomas Wolfe.
Copyright 1934, 1937, 1938, 1939, 1940
By Maxwell Perkins as Executor of the Estate of Thomas Wolfe.
Copyright renewed 1968 by Paul Gitlin.
Reprinted by permission of HarperCollins Publishers.

Editors: Christopher P. Cronin with Kathleen P. Cronin
Research: Beth-Ann Scott
Book Design: V. Gail Vonderweidt
Dust Jacket Art and Design: Abe Echevarria

Futura Press
457 Main Street
The Atrium, Suite 4A
Danbury, CT 06811

ISBN 0-9634254-0-4

Acknowledgments

This book is a tribute to the many people who suffered the pain of not knowing; a trophy to those who finally dared tell the truth.

To our spouses, who listened even when more pressing, personal problems threatened to steal away their attentions, we owe a great debt. Years ago Toni inspired a great beginning. She comforted and reassured when all hope of understanding had disappeared. Her inspiration has again ignited a comeback. Thank You.

And to Alvin and Jackie Brown, who show that faith, determination and dignity are essential to any renewal.

This book belongs to Sue Doyon as much as any of us. Her particular talents kept all the loose ends from becoming snarled knots. Beth-Ann Scott, a journalist who doggedly tracked down the meat and guts of this book, gave us the substance and grit we needed to tell a bold story. Chris Cronin, a historian with a conscience, deftly edited the manuscript though he mourned a recent sojourn in eastern Europe. His calls late at night or early in the morning, and Kathie's keen insight, always brought the project closer to the clear, concise work it became.

Doctors John Briggs and Carl Jensen are working journalists who truly understood our mission. Both nurtured this project in valuable ways. They understood this was more than another book, it was a new genre. Jensen wrote the forward despite his own deadline pressures; Briggs offered up his own contacts in publishing, putting his own great reputation as an author solidly behind us.

Gail Vonderweidt, who designed and produced these pages, did so with grace and love.

And finally, we thank all the people we interviewed, especially those who told us things that potentially could be damaging, personally or politically.

READER'S NOTE:

Style

There is great power in language. We have been aware of this fact for centuries, yet we still have no fool-proof defense against the attack of semantics. This is a disadvantage for people without unrelenting cynicism, or a complete knowledge of everything. Though some of us have more of the former than the latter, we still find ourselves lacking in the ability to find the truth behind words—especially when they are being used against us.

We have compiled a short list of words that are good examples of semantic weapons. These are old words with new meanings. Their new definitions have been created by the politicians and regulators who designed, executed and profited from a horrendously orchestrated savings and loan bailout. The definitions were changed so that regulators could operate under the guise of moral purpose. Allow us to illustrate.

Insolvent, overextended: These words had most often been used to describe a financial institution that owed an unrecoverable amount of money to people who invested with them. It is easy to change this definition so that a healthy, honest bank can look like a white collar crime ring. You do this by changing the definition of the ambiguous 'unrecoverable'. If a savings and loan had been allowed a capital-to-asset ratio of 2% and the rate jumps to 5% without warning, then any bank doing business at the old rate suddenly became a shyster. Citizens don't like shysters, and are happy when they pay for their sins. But its not so simple.

Non-performing loan: This is a tricky one, because it involves the public directly. A non-performing loan allows the holder of the loan to seize the collateral that was given as security. A non-performing loan is still that. What is different is that before the bailout, 'non-performing' actually meant, "payments are not being made on this loan." After the bailout began your loan could be reclassified as

Non-performing, even if the loan was being paid. It became "I don't care if these people haven't missed a payment in ten years, their bank is 'insolvent'" (use the new definition for this term...are you getting the picture?) So a homeowner may lose their home over this. And the scam escapes public scrutiny because everyone else is using the old definition of 'insolvent'. So what happens to the seized assets? Next definition.

Auction: We all know what an auction is. We all are familiar with bidding. Did we know that in the auctions run by the bailout brigade bids can go downward? What happens to the value of your home if your neighbor's house goes on their auction block because their bank has been "regulated"?

Qualified: Now means UNqualified—or qualified. Quite often, someone may try to buy land before it is foreclosed on for a price that is agreeable to the buyer and seller. The regulated bank, though, must approve such a sale. Often they refuse the sale because they have determined that a qualified buyer is indeed not qualified, and the property goes on the 'auction' block. And the bids can move downward.

Just think of the effect on the economy these few words can have. Actually, look at the want ads, the empty stores, the unemployment lines (ignore the official figures, by the way) and you'll have your "Economic Indicators."

Keep in mind as you read this book that you need to think twice about phrases and key words. There may be a wolf under that sheep's clothing.

"Let us build ourselves a city and a tower with its top in the heavens" - *The Descendants of Noah - Genesis 11, 4.*

"Let us go down, and there confuse their language so that they will not understand one another's speech." So the Lord scattered them from that place all over the earth; and they stopped building the city. For this reason it was called Babel, because there the Lord confused the speech of all the earth. - *Genesis 11, 7-9.*

FORM

Bailout is our contribution to a sorely needed, new genre in publishing—the serial non-fiction book.

As you read this largely unreported story about America and the economy, our editors, reporters and writers are already preparing a sequel. This is just the first of several books that will examine a contemporary story about our government and "What Went Wrong." This format allows us to publish solid books on issues that affect our lives rapidly.

The serial has long been a popular staple in fiction, especially among readers dating back to Sherlock Holmes, the Hardy Boys or the Nancy Drew mysteries. It was adopted by the film industry with mixed success and newspapers have always relied on the series to tell a long, complicated story.

But the serial is a new, hybrid in modern non-fiction. This new kid on the block has taken on some old traditions and has already gained a measure of critical and commercial success among readers (see forward). Journalists are supposed to protect the public's right to know, a sacred mission rarely taken up by book publishers. We feel it is a missed opportunity to adequately inform a public that would read books like this if only they were offered.

Hopefully, Bailout will serve that need. Employing traditional techniques of investigative journalism, we conducted numerous interviews with people in a position to know the story we wanted to tell. We also located damning, on-the-record testimonies and a wide range of government documents and investigations available to anyone who asked for them. In this way, we were able to document what we had long suspected—the bailout of American banks had been a miserable failure.

Surprisingly, the story we tell is new and still timely. But sadly, it is an unreported piece of contemporary American history you should have read about years earlier. This story is not the only one the media missed. As you will see in the following forward by Dr. Carl Jensen, these stories abound, just waiting to be packaged in the books we are already planning. The serial non-fiction book is a plum ripe for the picking, so we've plucked it. To tell stories about our time, in our time while the ending is still being written is an exciting prospect that once belonged to daily journalism. We've claimed it now. Wish us luck.

The Editors, August, 1992

CONTENTS

FORWARD

BAILOUT: The Bankrupting of America is a classic example of what modern-day muckrakers have to do to keep people better informed about the world around them. At the turn of the century, muckrakers like Lincoln Steffens and Ida Tarbell were able to have their investigative pieces published in daily newspapers and leading periodicals. Unfortunately, that is no longer true.

The banking crisis and it's victims is a story all Americans should know about because, like its sordid predecessor, the savings and loan crisis, all Americans are going to have to pay for the bailout. And yet the news media have once again failed to warn the public of the crisis.

Four years ago the press failed to cover the S&L crisis as it was building to a climax; not a single question about the S&L crisis and the pending bailout was asked during the three national political debates in 1988. It was only after the 1988 election that the politicians told the public it was going to have to pay hundreds of billions of dollars for the bailout.

Today, the financial scenario remains the same; only the names and the institutions have been changed. The politicians don't want to raise the subject because they're co-conspirators in the crime and once again no one in the media is asking the politicians about a bailout.

The establishment press avoids issues such as those raised in BAILOUT on the premise that they are too complex, too difficult to prove, too expensive to investigate, not to mention potentially embarrassing to their own shareholders and advertisers.

The media also avoids these issues because they don't fit what I call their Yo-Yo Formula for financial news—the stock market is up or down, the inflation rate is up or down, the prime rate is up or down, the bond market is up or down, the unemployment rate is up or down, the interest rate is up or down, the balance of payments is up or down, and gold, silver and pork bellies are up or down.

Reporting the nation's economy in a welter of disjointed yo-yo statistics may simplify it for the media, but it surely doesn't do much to inform the general public of what is really happening with the economy and how it affects your community.

The media's obsession with statistics was best seen in the weeks they spent publishing the endless rankings of the check bouncers in Congress. If the press had spent a tenth as much time and space on the national bank crisis as it did on the Congressional bank scandal, a solution would have been in the works by now.

But, most often the media will say they avoid financial stories because the public isn't interested. That, of course, is pure financial manure. Donald L. Bartlett and James B. Steele proved that people were interested in economic issues with their award-winning in-depth analysis of America's financial downfall, titled "America: What Went Wrong." The 1991 Philadelphia Inquirer series generated nearly a quarter million requests for reprints and was transformed into a national best-selling book in 1992.

Economics may indeed be the dismal science, but, in considering the impact it has on all our lives, it surely deserves better than the dismal coverage it gets from the media.

People are interested in issues that are relevant to their lives, issues that effect their pocketbooks, and issues that are told with conviction. And this is what Lionel Bascom and Richard DeSoto have done with BAILOUT. They believe in your right and need to know. And so do I.

Carl Jenson, Ph.D.
Project Censored
Sonoma State University
Rohnert Park, Ca. 94928
July, 1992

PROLOGUE

It is time to rethink the American Dream and our method of pursuit.

This book on its face is about the economy, banking and real estate, but it is really about people, how we behave when we ignore our actions, how it comes right back at us, even if we've followed all the rules (and perhaps precisely because we did).

Perhaps the real task of this book is to see the villain as something that we have not only accepted, but embraced. It is easier to always have a "them" to blame. It relieves us of our responsibility to stop ourselves, take our lumps, rethink, and start over. Put bluntly, we don't want to abandon the comfort of the status quo, no matter how misguided, to struggle and rebuild from the bottom up. As well, we don't want to look at our spouse, friend, child, parent, role-model, self as the reason why things have gone awry.

This book explores not so much the origins of a problem, but identifies the controllers at a floodgate. By letting others control our fortunes and destinies as this book describes, we have forfeited our country and our very lives.

"I believe we are lost here in America," Thomas Wolfe wrote in 1934, "but I believe we shall be found. And, this belief, which mounts now to the catharsis of knowledge and conviction, is for me—and I think for all of us—not only our hope, but America's everlasting, living dream."

Told in Richard DeSoto's voice, this book will take you through the research of DeSoto and Lionel Bascom as they expose elements of the savings and loan bailout. They show us who we left at the gate of the United States, and why it is so urgent to take that charge back.

1

THE NOTHING

In the fantasy novel, *The Neverending Story,* something mysterious was destroying the land of Fantastica.

The landscape was disappearing, being swallowed up by something its leaders could only call "The Nothing." People, even strong, powerful ones like the giant Rock Eater didn't die; they lost their strength and just faded away. No one knew how to stop it; no one knew why or how it was destroying this once bountiful landscape. The people of Fantastica just knew one thing—something was terribly wrong and they looked to their leaders to protect them.

A kind of Nothing had taken hold of the United States of America by the 1990's, an economic calamity no one in the American government seemed able to define clearly. Some were calling it a recession, but it had caused too much financial damage. It had infected too many lives and hurt too many people in too many places to have simply been a recession. All we seemed to know for sure was that wealth in America had begun to disappear. If it wasn't disappearing, it was certainly eluding us or worse, somehow, it was being transferred.

Even the most ordinary kinds of wealth, life as we knew it, the liberty even modest wealth allows, and the pursuit of happiness were vanishing. They were replaced by joblessness, homelessness and widespread economic chaos. Real estate values declined sharply, unemployment rose to twenty year highs, there were record numbers of bankruptcies, business failures, foreclosures and bank closings.

In rebuttal to critics who demanded that this uniquely American Nothing be named, there were the usual calls for a blind belief in the system; for patriotism and a public confidence that became as hard to find as jobs.

An example of this appeared in a letter to the New York Times on April 26, 1992. The writer told a true story about a bank in England that went bust sometime in the 1860s. A rumor had spread through the market town of Gloucestershire late on a Friday afternoon that it's only bank was failing. Angry depositors rushed the building and demanded their gold sovereigns.

The story, retold by Henry Ryland of Essex, Connecticut, reminded him of a similar one about a bank run in Kansas City earlier the same year. The story ran under the headline: "When Fear Takes Over: A Bank Run."

While the money in Kansas City had been backed by an American deposit insurance corporation, the English farmers in Gloucestershire hadn't been as fortunate.

As the story goes, some of the English depositors did not hear the rumor in time to withdraw their gold that black Friday. Nevertheless, everyone was assured they'd be paid in full on Monday.

"Come Monday morning," Ryland said, "the bank's window blinds were drawn up to show a large barrel heaped with gold sovereigns.

"The waiting crowd sighed with relief and most left satisfied that their funds were safe. The few who went inside were paid quickly.

"Years later, the truth came out; the barrel was not full of sovereigns, but had been upended and the few sovereigns the bank was able to obtain were heaped in a cone on top of the barrel's bottom. Confidence—though misplaced—had been restored," Ryland said. The illusion had worked.

One hundred and thirty years later, that same kind of illusion was used by our government in a decidedly more serious, if not similar occasion. Instead of one bank, however, there were hundreds of troubled banks throughout the United States.

Like the English bank, the U.S. government knew it could not allow public confidence in American banking institutions to fail. Ryland's story aptly described what came to be known as the banking bailout of the late 1980s and early 1990s in America.

Americans from the coast of Maine to the Pacific Palisades knew that banks throughout our country were on shaky financial ground; we knew that our economy had fallen to unprecedented lows; and we also knew that the federal government had assured us, by enacting a variety of sweeping legislative measures, that our money was safe. There would be no black Friday for depositors in America.

There was, however, another parallel that had gone almost completely unnoticed. Put in the simplest terms possible, the people in both stories were the victims of deliberate illusions aimed at gaining their confidence.

"These illusions have cost us time and money," one House of Representatives investigation late in 1991 said, two years after a comprehensive bank bailout plan engineered by the White House was enacted.

While American's were told repeatedly that their deposits

were insured; the value of their real estate—their homes, businesses and farms—was rapidly being eroded away by the same agents that Congress had put in charge of America's assets.

I knew what had been going on as a result of nearly three years of research while trying to save my own real estate business. I contacted Lionel Bascom, a journalism professor at Western Connecticut State University in Danbury, Connecticut. I hoped he could help me write what I had been calling a book on banking. He called me in the spring of 1992 and we decided to collaborate immediately. You see, he had arrived at the same conclusion six months earlier—something was wrong.

Lionel's first indication of this Nothing which seemed to be spoiling the ground we walked on, came from Prof. Carl Jensen, founder of Project Censored at Sonoma State University in California. For sixteen years, Jensen's project singled out the "Ten Most Censored Stories" in an annual review of the media. In 1991, the banking scandal was named among them.

As Lionel and I started comparing notes, we realized something: for the first time, the Nothing we had both been wrestling with had a name—it was variously called banking reform or the S&L bailout. While the sins of the Savings and Loan scandal were widespread, the ensuing economic catharsis that was caused by our government was not common knowledge.

In separate investigations, Lionel Bascom and I both began to pursue this story. As a real estate syndicator and builder who developed multi-million dollar real estate projects, I personally knew some of the casualties. When one of my banks closed, I began to see the wider problem and how it was tied directly to legislation enacted to solve economic problems, not create them.

What we learned was far different from the scenario being played out in the press. While some people had always dismissed

Jensen and his Project Censored as just the work of a liberal academic, he had clearly zeroed in on one of the most cancerous dilemmas of our time.

Legislative remedies to shore up an ailing banking industry, at least in part, had caused further economic erosion across the nation.

Lionel's twenty years of experience as a newsman, writer and teacher of journalism had taught him there was more to the so—called banking story than he knew. Something was radically wrong with our economy and whatever it was, it wasn't being widely or thoroughly reported. He knew there was an upturned barrel somewhere that had been topped with gold sovereigns to instill confidence. What he did not know was where.

We agreed that governments deftly manipulated the news, but it was usually accomplished by omissions, not by lying. A lie was too confining; it was a trap that could suddenly be sprung open by almost any enterprising reporter who simply checked their facts. Omissions, on the other hand, left the government with an escape route, a technique which came into widespread use during the presidency of Richard Nixon. It became known as plausible denial.

Forgetting was a plausible and pardonable sin; lying was not.

There were a number of upturned barrels to explain our ailing economy in the 1990s and wherever we looked at the beginning of that decade, they all seemed plausible. Banks had made too many bad loans. America had embraced the faulty idea of becoming a service economy and wound up with too many minimum wage jobs. Manufacturing had gone overseas. Collective bargaining agreements weren't worth the paper they had been written on anymore. And, many banks were overextended. While we were assured that our deposits were safe, we were also shown the high-rollers in the savings and loan scandal who were being hunted down by federal prosecutors. Some of the bankers who had bought yachts, Rolls Royces, luxury homes with depositor's and stockholder's funds were jailed. A sentiment that was widely shared throughout America was that bankers who plundered shareholder or depositor's funds belonged in jail.

But still, something seemed out of whack. With so many upended barrels, so many complicated financial details to absorb, it was difficult to know what that something was. Savings were rescued; the bad guys were going to jail and the Congress seemed to labor over one prescriptive law after another aimed at preventing massive bank failures from happening again.

Together, it made deciphering an already complicated story almost impossible.

By 1992, something was threatening to sink my business. I had fended off what I considered undeserved attacks by bankers, federal regulators and their lawyers who were trying to seize everything I owned. When my banks were closed, a noose fashioned from a tangled web of new federal laws, government regulations and scared bankers was wrapped tightly around my neck. I could lose my home, my business, and a long—standing reputation in my community built in part by reliably paying my bills.

My life and work had been what we traditionally call the American Dream. The irony of my dilemma was that I fell victim to the very rules by which I had always played.

Rising from a boyhood that began on welfare in a tawdry Massachusetts public housing project, I had built a profitable business along with my wife, Toni. I believed in "The System" until this Nothing descended upon me. When it threatened to take everything, my survivor's instincts made me want to fight it. But first, I had to learn what this Nothing was, and learn how to beat it.

As Lionel and I discovered, the bank bailout was a scandal of equal proportion to the S&L crisis that had spawned it. It was one of the best kept, secret bungles in America.

2

THE ATRIUM

Even I didn't understand it immediately when the tentacles of what they were politely calling a recession threatened to ruin my business and life.

I was a player, a dealer in the high stakes game of real estate development and banking. I had never missed a loan payment, had always maintained impeccable credit and was rewarded handsomely with the spoils of my own hard work. If I could drive a luxury car, it was because I sweated over a development deal ten years earlier that had worked. If I could afford to send my daughter to Wooster, a posh private school, it was because I was not only willing to take my commissions, I was also willing to move a single mother into the house I had sold to her.

Twenty five years and millions of dollars in real estate deals later had made me wealthy by almost anybody's standards. Still, I too found myself on the brink of bankruptcy.

Back in the late 1950's, my father worked as a truck driver earning $57 a week. When my parents tried to move the family from the tenement where we lived to a modest development of new duplex homes called Mill Ridge, they were turned down because they couldn't scrape up the $500 down payment.

We spent our vacations visiting relatives in Rhode Island or swimming at the Town Park, a public beach.

Three decades later, just a few miles from Mill Ridge, I had built a three million dollar brick office building that I called The Atrium, where I ran my businesses. My wife, Toni and our children now vacationed in Maine at our oceanfront, three bedroom second home.

Why should anybody care about my bankruptcy? For two reasons. First, if this could happen to someone as careful as I'd been, working my way up as I had done, it could happen to anyone. But more importantly, Americans need to know what caused this to happen. It was no accident.

Over the years, I had carefully plugged myself into circles of friends and associates who dealt the cards of success to one another. The game was played at lunch among players like me; men who's business education came from real experience. I was one of the founders of the Young Republicans Club in my town during the Nixon years. I had voted for George Bush and had supported conservative causes. I believed that greed was ruining America and wrote letters to my congressional representatives, saying so. I believed in the system, played by the rules and considered anyone who attacked our government a subversive.

That's what I once believed.

If pursuing the American Dream led someone into bankruptcy, I knew something had gone terribly wrong, something no one was reporting. For now, I'll call it "the plan" and it was being executed swiftly across America by mid 1991. That summer, I spent weeks getting legal advice. The news was not good.

By the middle of August, I was so upset at the idea of losing everything after one meeting with lawyers, my body shivered as I left my attorney's office and drove north through one of the most affluent corners of America—Fairfield County, Connecticut. My head ached and I had terrible stomach cramps. I had difficulty seeing because I cried all the way home to Danbury, still a working class Connecticut town once known as the Hat City of the world.

As a kid, any wealth the hating industry brought to Danbury wasn't always evident to me. I lived in a blue collar neighborhood in the center of town populated by a mixture of Portuguese, Italian and other immigrants who had come there to find work. Thousands of immigrants came to Danbury from European countries like Hungary after revolution had destroyed it in the 1950's.. Thousands of poor blacks also moved north to cities like Danbury and Bridgeport to work. I was too young to understand exactly what happened, but when the hating industry died like many industries in the Rust Belt of northern cities in the late 1960's, it had a devastating effect on people's lives.

Twenty years later, when "the plan" hit us, news commentators were calling it a recession—a limp word for what I was seeing. I watched my friends fall one by one. It strangled real estate, banking, retail sales, construction and had a rippling effect on other businesses throughout the region. The hospital was laying off nurses; X-ray technicians couldn't even find part-time work. Consultants and unemployed corporate types consoled one another in weekly group therapy sessions because none of them could find work anymore. The only "downturn" people really understood were the responses they were getting when they looked for jobs.

While it was a difficult story to report, it was not the scrambled bunch of facts and figures reported in the media. It was also not the cyclical, temporary business downturn the administration in Washington had led us to believe it was.

For me, it began in the fall of 1990. Two years earlier, my bank, CityTrust, had extended a $1 million line of credit to me and said I could spend this borrowed money any way I saw fit. American business runs on the strength of its lines of credit. In September of 1990, I was planning projects that I had intended to finance with my new credit line, something I had been told by my bank I could count on.

I was structuring a delicate deal that required cash. In an attempt to reduce the debt I had incurred building the Atrium, I planned to turn its 24,000 square feet into condominiums and sell off the units. To accomplish this, I needed a 2% reduction in the interest rate I had been paying, a routine request for good customers in the past. I also wanted another $150,000 to offset expenditures I needed to turn the Atrium rental space into condominiums. Keith Posner, my banker, didn't even nod at my request, he just processed the paperwork and told me to wait. Later, when I queried Keith again about what I had been repeatedly told was routine business, he began to talk in circles.

Remember, I had never defaulted on any loan. Over the years, I had repaid CityTrust millions in loans, sometimes paying interest as high as 22 percent. By all definitions, I was a good credit risk. This time, there was a snag. When I asked Keith what was holding up the approval, he first told me he did not know.

On the street and in restaurants over lunch, people complained about the officers at CityTrust, saying they were suddenly refusing loans to longtime, paying customers. Even worse, people were saying they were calling in loans and pressuring borrowers with unreasonable demands for updated financial statements.

But these guys had courted my business. In fact, the way I got my first million dollar credit line back in 1988 began as a joke. When I went in to conduct one transaction or another, bank officers repeatedly asked me what they could do to get all of my business.

"Give me a million dollar line," I said jokingly. Four weeks later, I paid a $10,000 fee and got the line. It blew me away. I could easily dismiss the CityTrust rumors.

If they were refusing loans or calling loans, the customers were probably deadbeats who deserved to be pressured.

I borrowed by the book. I had more than $250,000 deposited in CityTrust. My request for a lower interest rate on my current loans and an additional loan was routine. I told Keith that I planned on paying the entire loan off by selling a quarter of the Atrium each year.

When they asked for a new financial statement and a new appraisal, I complied. I spent the $2,500 it cost and sent what they wanted over and waited. Then something began to go haywire.

The day before the bank's loan committee was supposed to hear my request for the extra $150,000, the request was pulled and never brought before the committee. Keith was supposed to make the presentation. When I asked him why he hadn't, he dodged the question.

I called a meeting with Jim Murphy, Keith's boss.

"You aren't getting the 2% interest rate reduction or the $150,000," Murphy said. "In fact, you aren't getting your million dollar credit line renewed either."

Just sixty days earlier, Keith told me the credit line had been approved. One of them was lying or had lied. Keith, who sat in on that meeting, told his boss the line had been approved.

"I am not approving it," Murphy countered, unless you give me more collateral.

Then he told me the bank wouldn't lend me a nickel until I spent the $250,000 I had in accounts there to reduce the previous $1 million I had borrowed.

I still wanted to borrow by the book. The problem I was now facing, however, was the fact that Jim and Keith were apparently following rules from books I had never seen. I had wasted four months waiting for what had seemed like a routine deal to solidify and spent thousands of dollars trying to comply with new appraisals, and financial statements, not knowing I was giving aid and comfort to the enemy. The government had changed the rules.

Every time I tried to nail down the deal by providing these bankers I had done business with for twenty years with new paperwork, the loan seemed to slip further and further out of reach. It was like nailing down Jell-O.

It took a while to sink in but Murphy was threatening to call my previous million dollar loan. First he'd take the cash I had deposited in his bank, then I was sure he'd go after the money I had in other banks. They could also attach any real estate I owned and keep me from selling it. I had set out to secure a loan and wound up fighting these bastards to save everything I owned.

For the next six months, I spent every waking hour trying to protect my ~~ass~~ not selling or maintaining the real estate I owned. In May, I visited George Taylor, chief executive officer of CityTrust. He was cordial but nervous. We had been friends for years and we both knew it during that awful meeting. He said there was nothing he could do, the bank was under orders from the Federal Deposit Insurance Corporation. This was puzzling because the FDIC was an underwriter of deposits, not in charge of loans. At least that's what I mistakenly believed. It is my belief that God put us on this planet for one reason and one reason only. He put us here to help each other. This thought puts you at ill ease when friends resign their care to a bureaucratic arrangement they won't help you fight.

In August, all hell broke loose when they did call my million-dollar loan. They also froze my accounts, including one in which I had deposited $25,000 the week before to cover bills and commissions. Checks bounced all week.

Adding insult to injury, a messenger delivered a three page document from CityTrust to my office on a Friday with more outrageous demands. Among them was a request that I sign over all my properties immediately as collateral or they'd foreclose on my office building and my house on Monday. The document looked legal enough but to check, I called George Taylor.

"Mr. Taylor has resigned," the secretary told me.

Instead, I found myself in front of a committee of strangers at the bank. "We want new appraisals," they said. "We want to know how much money you have and which banks are holding it. We also want to know the names of everyone in your profit sharing plan. We want your general partnership agreement, we want all the leases on your real estate. "We want," they kept saying, and I was one of the bank's best paying customers. That's why I had gotten the million-dollar line of credit in the first place, remember.

"What are you after?" I demanded.

"Your loan has been called because it's a non performing loan," one of them told me, using a term that was generally used for dead-beats.

"How can that be," I countered. "I've never missed a payment, not even once."

"The bank has over extended itself to you, Mr. DeSoto, they lent you too much money and we're worried you won't be able to make the notes." "If I was going anywhere, would I have deposited $25,000 in your bank or left over $20,000 in my profit sharing plan?"

I left that meeting with a week to produce all the information they wanted on me. The next day, I read a news story about a lawsuit in which someone had sued CityTrust. Later, federal regulators came to town and closed CityTrust down.

I didn't know it then, but my nightmare had only just begun.

3

Downward Mobility

Understanding exactly when the American economy bottomed out depended on which economic indicator you believed in, real estate, unemployment or the stock market. Something had gone wrong by the early 90's and we began to feel its effects in widely divergent sections of the country.

Whatever it was that halted a seemingly endless prosperity of the 1980's, it came crashing down squarely into the living rooms of every American who watched television news by 1992.

Night after night, commentators delivered the bad news, speaking in tongues only those steeped in economic jargon could really understand. Housing starts? Dow Jones Industrial Average? Trillion dollar budget deficits? What did it all mean to us and more importantly, how much was all of this going to cost? No one seemed to know. The Bush Administration stalled, forecasting prosperity in an election year when even the indicators they used could not accurately explain to the average American what had happened to our economy. In the months preceding the 1992 presidential election, the nightly news began sounding the alarm that the economy had "ticked up" by tenths of percentage points in this sector or that market.

It didn't make sense to people who could not find jobs, or to businesses who could no longer borrow or find customers to buy what they were selling.

Something was up, something larger than almost anything my baby boomer generation had experienced before. The ranks of the homeless were being joined in large numbers by sober, unemployed men, women and children.

It was something so simple, something so fundamental, even a freshman economics major might have been able to spot it. Something pivotal happened in the late 1980's, something that was started by our government that went awry and it was at least partly responsible for sending the U.S. economy careening downward and out of control by the early 1990's. You'll remember it as the recession of that decade but it was far worse than anything anyone reading the newspapers at the time knew. Sure, it was dubbed one of the Ten Most Censored Stories of 1991, but still the media missed the significance of what government bank regulators were doing to our already frail economy.

Despite the jumbled, and often confusing reports of the worst economic times in sixty years, the widespread economic woes we began to suffer in the late 1980's and early 1990's might have been better explained if reporters had examined why so many businesses suddenly went under. Instead, they reported what they were told was the real story—a cyclical "downturn" in the economy. It was like calling cancer a temporary disruption in normal bodily function. The signs were everywhere, starting with the United States Congress and evident in every corner of America by 1992.

A handful of political appointees and their army of young civil servants, lawyers, Realtors and real estate appraisers had carried out one of the largest corporate takeovers in American history. Armed with regulations from the Financial Institutions Reform, Recovery and Enforcement Act of 1989, two government agencies became the largest, single owners of more commercial and residential real estate in the U.S. than any other single entity. First, the Federal Deposit Insurance Corporation moved in and audited banks. They were followed by the Resolution Trust Corporation (RTC), which either shut the bank down or took possession of its assets, repackaged them and resold them to sounder institutions. Together, these agencies targeted up to one thousand of the almost 13,000 banks across the country. These regulators swept through whole regions of the country, systematically shutting down what it termed as insolvent banks, and scooping up billions of dollars in assets in the process.

But savings and loan institutions weren't the only kinds of banks the RTC went after. Among the banks FDIC and RTC officials said were insolvent were some of the nation's largest commercial banks. While the Congress kept a list of these banks secrets, the RTC moved swiftly. Technically, they never held title to any of the assets they seized. Nevertheless, they acted as if they owned the vast wealth the Congress had ordered them to liquidate. This extensive transfer of what had once been private property took less than three years.

On the heels of the savings and loan scandal of the 1980's and the faltering economy that followed in the next decade, these U.S. regulators began a sweeping plan that may eventually alter commercial banking and the way we do business in America for decades to come.

Bank regulators and examiners, credited with saving taxpayer's deposits by closing banks and savings and loan institutions, also cut off large segments of the population from needed loans and lines of credit. Bankruptcies climbed to record heights; foreclosures became common throughout the country. Seized real estate, billions of dollars worth of properties that had been people's homes and businesses, were discounted and resold. This had a devastating, but seldom reported effect on the economy.

While it had become clear by 1990 that many banks were in deep financial trouble, the way in which this problem was handled sent financial shock waves throughout the U.S. like jolts of electricity.

When an institution fell into their hands, it was the bank's good customers with paid up loans and credit lines that ultimately took the brunt of their wrath, not depositors.

While these agencies publicly touted themselves as saviors of taxpayer deposits, the Federal Deposit Insurance Corporation and The Resolution Trust Corporation systematically discounted the value of real estate by as much as 50 percent in communities across the country in an attempt to liquidate the acquired assets of failed banks.

Caught in this maze of red tape and paperwork, thousands of paying customers who had never missed a loan payment were snared and ordered by these federal liquidators to pay off large loans. Thirty day notices from banks or federal agencies demanding huge sums were almost always followed by liens that kept homeowners or businessmen from selling their liquid assets. Commercial real estate loans were called overnight. Well run, sound businesses were suddenly hurled into bankruptcy.

For the first time in anyone's memory, owning real estate became the one vehicle that could drive millions of ordinary people and businesses into bankruptcy.

This was an important slice of American history, a missing piece that finally helped explain why our economy faltered in the 90's and nobody seemed to know how to fix it.

4

GROUND ZERO

I began working on the Atrium in the spring of 1986. It was the largest single building project of my career. When the builing was dedicated, men still pushed wheel barrels while heavy equipment moved into place to pour the foundation. The mayor of my small town, James Dyer, showed up to commemorate the occasion.

I was a card carrying, tax paying businessman in this community and many of the people I had worked with over the years showed up to celebrate the occasion. In a small town like Danbury, even radio and newspaper reporters came out to cover a piece of the town's economic progress.

For the city it meant jobs, increased water and tax revenues and a sign that our economy was still growing. As a businessman, I had done my homework and knew that I could fully rent my office space. My building would not become one of those many empty office towers like those in Texas.

I tossed the keys to my old office into the newly poured concrete that sunny afternoon in April, and a project I had only dreamed of for years got underway. Indeed, the future looked pretty good for the boy from a Fall River, Massachusetts housing project.

The interest payments on my new project began to come in almost immediately, something all developers have to contend with to complete their projects. First the payments were $10,000 a month, then they climbed to $15,000 reaching a height of $20,000 each month.

One day, I spent six hours on the phone with my attorney to iron out problems with the general contractor. Those calls continued through the evening and I wound up talking to him on my car phone while I waited outside my daughter's school where she was playing basketball. I also negotiated a lease with a new tenant over the phone that night. By the time my daughter, Christina, finally came out, the battery in my car had gone dead.

These hours paid off. I got the tenant and my lawyer had assured me my contract problems would not interfere with construction. There were numerous other problems along the way, including a leaky roof, more fights with contractors, subcontractors, swarms of lawyers and many others. Nevertheless, eighteen months later, The Atrium was ready for tenants.

Five years later, I still had not missed a single mortgage payment, though I was in danger of losing not only the Atrium, but all of my other holdings. When CityTrust closed in August 1991, everything I owned was almost suddenly put in jeopardy.

I learned that CityTrust had closed one Saturday when the newsboy delivered the morning paper. I read the story in the driveway of my house where the paper fell. CityTrust was now Chase Manhattan, an out-of-state bank.

I had lived in that house for nineteen years, taught my daughters to ride tricycles in that same driveway; watched my wife, Toni, agonize over where she should plant that two-foot high dogwood tree. My daughters are now sixteen and nineteen; the tree has grown to twenty feet.

All my wrangling with the people I had known at CityTrust had been fruitless. I knew now I'd have to offer up my pleas to a gang of New York boys who took over my bank. To make matters worse, the shots were really being called by bean counters in Washington, people who had probably never sold a single, square foot of real estate in their lives.

I knew I was in for a bad time, but had no idea just how bad it would get until a year later.

About the same time, Robert L. Clarke, Comptroller Of The Currency and also board member of the Federal Deposit Insurance Corporation and member of the RTC board, took New England by storm. Under Clarke's direction, regulators reclassified billions of dollars in loans, shifting once acceptable loans like mine into piles of what they were now calling non-performing loans. There was a new world order all right and everybody running it was insane.

From a source inside the FDIC, I learned that the regulators who came to Connecticut were from the southwest. For the first time, I realized what it must have been like for Southerners when the carpetbaggers from the north descended upon them after the Civil War. Looking at my house that afternoon, for the first time I really understood the scene in "Gone With the Wind" when Scarlett O'Hara says, "I'll never go hungry again." As a kid, I had been hungry and remember the five of us once sharing a peck of potatoes for a month.

People I didn't know would be coming after me; I knew they'd try to take my house, my business. Under ordinary circumstances, I could fight them—pit my lawyers against their lawyers—and survive.

But the game I was suddenly hurled into had no rules that I understood. In business, most situations are negotiable. Would these new guys negotiate?

I decided my best defense was to first learn what I was up against and began my awakening through back channels at the FDIC. What I learned scared the hell out of me.

My source, who asked to remain anonymous for fear of reprisals, told me that New England banks would be devastated and the economy here would suffer unprecedented losses. They planned to close at least 60 banks in a single year in Connecticut alone. Hinting that this situation could be lucrative for those who knew what was coming, my source laid out how loans were handled, shocking me even further.

"Why would anyone in their right mind repackage and discount performing loans for new buyers?" I asked him during one of the many late night telephone calls we had that summer.

"They have to unload as many loans as possible so they can go before Congress and ask for more operating money," he said. "They have to show they are resolving the banking crisis and by selling off a closed bank's loans, it appears they are resolving bad loans and putting good loans into the responsible hands of new bankers," I was told. "They're closing banks so fast, they cannot keep up with the number of loans they have to process," my source said. Although I did not know it at the time, my source was talking about billions of dollars in loan portfolios. I only began to understand what he meant after I visited a regional FDIC office in our state capital, Hartford.

Lined up on the floor and stacked three deep in some cases were boxes and boxes of unprocessed loans this office had to deal with one way or another. I knew these files represented thousands of people who suddenly found themselves in the same position I now found myself in. While the Congress told these regulators to liquidate these loans, they did not know that these regulators were throwing away paying customers like me along with the truly bad loans at the banks they closed. It was insanity for those of us whose lives were suddenly being thrown away in cardboard boxes. For the FDIC, it was the most expedient way to get the job done.

The loans of failed banks were being resold to a wide range of buyers at deep discounts. These would include both performing loans like mine and the non-performing loans.

You could buy a twelve percent performing loan discounted up to 20 cents on the dollar and that package had already been discounted by an unknown amount. Fortunes were being made because these loans were again resold overnight by the sellers who were netting high returns on investment.

I was among the poor ~~bastards~~ being asked to pay off a $1 million note or lose everything. If I didn't find the money or at least renegotiate the terms, I was going to wind up in bankruptcy. In better times, someone with my financial history could have easily borrowed the money I needed so desperately now, but, all the banks I had relationships with had gone under. Some of the banks that were still standing, did not have time to conduct their usual business. They were also too busy fending off regulators who were trying to close them down.

I was told to expect a letter soon telling me to either continue paying my note or to pay it off, then I'd be told where to send my money. It would be an address I would not be familiar with nor would there be a person with whom I could discuss my portfolio. While we were celebrating the end of Communist Socialism around the world, the United States was experiencing its own transfer of wealth.

Nine months later, I got six registered letters from a law firm calling my million dollar loan. No one had contacted me to discuss this loan. Unless I could do something, I'd be forced into bankruptcy.

A short time later, a sheriff dropped by my office, serving me with a thick legal document that meant a lien had been attached to all of my real estate. After living on ulcer medication for months, lying awake nights trying to calculate my way out of an impossible situation, the legal game had finally begun.

I checked and double checked everything I had done over the last year in an attempt to protect my assets. Did I miss something or would they be able to move in and take my house? My days and nights were now consumed with surviving. When I listened to the news now, I wondered when this nightmare I was going through would become a news story. For a brief period, I wanted to believe someone had just made a mistake in my case. I knew better. I knew it was happening to others but so far, they had just been files in boxes I had seen in that Hartford office. Then my friends began to drop like flies from the same plague I was battling.

When I finally realized just how widespread these attacks were, I knew I was involved in some huge, national conspiracy. Even more significantly, I realized that my story and the stories of thousands—maybe even millions like me—might never be told. The mainstream media had already begun reporting the demise of the 1992 recession. Bush was running for reelection and as I watched television broadcasts in the months preceding his second run at the White House, the media seemed to have no idea how deeply troubled the economy was then or how long it would take to be revived. That's when I decided to write this book.

I owned a house not twenty minutes from Bush's in

Kennebunkport, Maine. I used to delight in the fact that one day I might sit on my ocean-view, front porch and watch the President's cigarette boat cruise by. I had agreed with this President and voted for him because I too wanted to protect all of the things he and the conservatives of this country said they wanted to protect. I used to drive friends down to the Bush compound and brag about my neighbor, the President." Now, the people I had always supported, the people Ronald Reagan and Bush had appointed were coming after me, trying to take it all away.

"While our economy may be beset by difficulty it should not be beset with doubt."
— President George Bush, February, 1990

5

THE FIRST HUNDRED DAYS

Ever since the whirl-wind first hundred days of Franklin D. Roosevelt Presidency, political scientists and speculators have learned to measure the future of a new president by his performance within this time frame.

The current wisdom dictates that if the political speculator can capture the essence of the first 100 days of any president; the mood conveyed, the priorities given, the legislation developed, that speculator has a crystal ball.

It becomes easy to see what the rest of that president's term will yield. In Roosevelt's case, his first hundred days saw the development of the New Deal—a radical approach to government's role in economy—spelling a volatile future for America under his leadership.

Truman's first hundred days brought us the end of the Second World War in a way that profoundly changed war and diplomacy. Eisenhower showed us that we were in for a period of numb serenity.

After a hundred days of George Bush, the critics had mixed anticipation. Some were very pleased at how easily his first budget was passed. Some were skeptical about his seeming confirmation of what he repeatedly had said up to days before his inauguration; that he had no agenda for his presidency.

To examine Bush's presidency, though, we must look at how well prepared he was for his first term as chief executive.

Critics who charged that George Bush had been a weak domestic President during his first term in office had failed to recognize a single, calculated risk he took in the first weeks of his presidency. Bush was sworn into office late in January of 1989. By February, the newly installed Bush Administration had moved a sweeping piece of domestic legislation from the White House to the floors of the Senate and the House of Representatives. It was a comprehensive piece of legislation designed to shore up America's failing banking industry.

By several accounts, the bill written to fix these problems rode smoothly through the Senate, passing on April 19th during Bush's first three months as president.

"In extraordinarily quick fashion, the Senate ... gave overwhelming approval to the most sweeping reform of the nation's savings and loan regulatory structure since it was established in the 1930s," a Washington-based weekly reported.

"Bush and the advocates of tighter control on thrifts (savings banks) won virtually every major fight," the Congressional Quarterly said.

The House version passed with relatively little debate and became law in August of the same year.

But several questions arose once the one thousand page bank salvage bill was signed by the President. A major one concerned the economy. When the legislation was written, the administration knew its success would be heavily dependent upon economic factors which they might not be able to control.

When Bush signed the House bill on August 9, 1989, the administration hoped for favorable economic growth and that interest rates and thrift deposits would climb by at least five percent a year. Instead interest rates and deposits fell and the economy soured.

In turn, federal bank regulators who were sent into the failing thrifts began reclassifying thousands of performing loans into non-performing loans almost overnight, forcing many companies and individuals to file bankruptcy.

The combined debt of failed companies in 1990 alone went up an estimated $65 billion, up 80 percent from the previous year. According to Dun and Bradstreet, bankruptcy in 1990 increased by 21 percent over 1989 by 60,000.

The American Bankruptcy Institute conducted a survey in 1991 that estimated that bankruptcies would be up to one million by the end of 1992. The largest increase was found in New England where 92 percent of the bankruptcies were filed by individuals.

President Bush's first proposal to spend $157.6 billion through 1999 to close 350 plus insolvent savings and loan associations was met with serious concern, not only from taxpayers, but also from the American Bankers Association.

The taxpayers who had questioned the cost to the average citizen to clean up the thrift industry formed a coalition dubbed the "financial democracy campaign." The Rev. Jesse Jackson, who joined the coalition on March 2, 1989 to attack Bush's plan, estimated that the cost of the plan over time could be as high as $1,000 per family.

Bush's bill to overhaul insolvent thrifts was called the Financial Institutions Reform, Recovery and Enforcement Act or (FIRREA), it shut down the Federal Savings and Loan Insurance

Corporation (FSLIC), which had bank savings and loan deposits and created a new depositors fund for thrifts under the Federal Depositors Insurance Corporation (FDIC).

Two off-budget agencies were also formed because of the FIRREA bill. One, the RTC to take over insolvent thrifts and either close them or sell them off, while at the same time managing and selling assets that were once held by the once solvent thrifts. The RTC was designed to go out of business no later than December 31, 1996. The second off-budget agency, FSLIC Resolution Fund, set up to sell $50 billion in bonds to finance the closures of the bankrupt thrifts.

Bush originally wanted the costs off budget to keep it from adding to the growing federal deficit.

The RTC has already been given an additional sum amounting to more than $100 billion to close insolvent thrifts and to dispose of assets the thrifts once held.

By May of 1992, the RTC reported that there were no bank closings because the agency had run out of funds. The RTC had closed 651 thrifts, more than twice the number planned for in the Bush strategy. One inquiry two years after the bailout began, said three times as many institutions could fail. How could so many banks be failing? How could our government not have known how deeply this plan would cut into one of the most vital industries in the nation? What almost no one was saying had become obvious to a few who had examined the bank bailout. It had failed, cutting deep gashes into our economy along the way.

6

Government's Barrel

When the Financial Institutions Reform, Recovery and Enforcement Act became law, the largest asset takeover in American history got underway under the noses of a bungling Congress and an unwary press. When government agents began to close down troubled banks, media coverage surrounding one of the biggest fiscal cleanups generally concentrated on the FDIC's saving of depositors' funds.

This was a useful illusion. Few people lost their savings in a modern version of the upended barrel. Whenever the shade was drawn up on the bank bailout, we saw government agents—the guys in the white hats—shutting down what they called insolvent banks to save depositor's passbook accounts. Our sovereigns were safe.

Between the years 1989 and 1992, the Congress repeatedly passed banking legislation with confidence—building names like Financial Institutions Reform, Recovery, and Enforcement Act or the Financial Recovery Act. Nevertheless, something fundamental had begun to chew up the American economy. Texas fell. New

England followed. It swept through California like the Santa Ana winds. Still, almost no one linked this sudden fiscal chaos to a plan to close banks throughout America, a far more radical plan than it first seemed to most observers.

Early in that decade, while Communist governments were giving up state ownership of whole nations around the world, the U.S. government had quietly begun to take over and control hundreds of billions of dollars in once valuable real estate and other assets across America.

While most depositor's were spared the loss of their life savings, tens of thousands of other paying bank customers were driven into bankruptcy. By the summer of 1992, the federal government also controlled more rental property than any entity in the country.

By the early 1990's the Berlin Wall and the Soviet Union were crumbling. Meanwhile, an enthusiastic takeover of private property sponsored by the quasi-governmental RTC was running full-steam.

Begun under the guise of a cleanup of the troubled banking industry, government agencies seized at least $350 billion in assets—taking it from citizens who held mortgages and loans.

The takeover artists were a mix of hastily trained, sincere but young regulators; highly paid lawyers, questionable appraisers, Realtors and wealthy speculators who together began to control vast portfolios of bank assets. All worked on behalf of the RTC.

These holdings had once belonged to people who lost everything despite the fact they had always maintained solid credit and had always paid their mortgages. The RTC also took possession of more than 70,000 rental properties. In some instances, their lawyers hauled dozens of tenants into court and attempted wholesale evictions. Joseph Kennedy, the Democratic congressman from

Massachusetts said this occurred in far flung parts of the country.

While the Congress quibbled over the fictive costs of regulating the banking industry after decades of sanctioned deregulation—hundreds of billions of dollars in real estate was sold off at deep discounts like second hand clothing to individuals, large corporations and holding companies who began making fortunes overnight.

The assumption that these holdings belonged to corrupt bank officers, unscrupulous developers and speculators, was widespread. It was also dead wrong.

The government, with little business experience or background in either real estate, real estate banking, or land-owning suddenly had the largest holdings in two of the most profitable industries in the nation. If the property they seized had belonged solely to bank pirates and deadbeat borrowers, it might have been viewed as a responsible act.

But overnight, regulators began the reclassification of paying loans into non-performing loans. These portfolios represented the homes and businesses of good customers as well as delinquents.

When a bank was closed, an untallied number of these loans were just called and borrowers who had always paid their bills were suddenly ordered to pay off their $150,000 home mortgages; settle up $30,000 in up-to-date credit lines, or worse. Many of these loans were demand notes, which means they could be called with 30 days notice. The large number of these called had a sudden and devastating impact on the economy. Profitable businesses had to pay off million dollar loans even though their owners had never missed a payment.

All of this had a disastrous effect on the economy. But then, the government made a bad situation even worse by dumping hundreds of homes, condominiums and commercial tracts of real estate back on the market with deep discounts. Real estate values plummeted everywhere. Local tax revenues for the properties the RTC held went largely unpaid once the original owners either declared bankruptcy or turned the property over to the RTC managers. The costs were incalculable.

7

No Chip Poker

I had become the unwitting victim of a high stakes game decidedly did not want to play. The federal government was stacking the deck against me and millions of other unsuspecting people like me.

The question I kept asking the lawyers I had hired to defend me was "why?" At the time, my lawyers didn't understand what was happening to me because the laws were changing too fast.

One of the greatest myths of the decade had to be the illusion projected by our government that they were saving us from a nation of bad bankers. It had been a carefully orchestrated plan to bypass congressional and state legislative mandates against interstate banking.

In one respect, the plan worked. Out-of-state banks began popping up in states across the country without benefit of law. They swooped down and bought the assets of failed banks with the help and the blessing of federal regulators.

In a more important respect, however, the plan backfired, knocking out vital underpinnings tied to an economy already weakened by a decade of wild borrowing and investment schemes that had gone bad. Cloaked in the anti-bank sentiments of the time, public feelings created when the nation learned that savings and loans had squandered billions in bad loans to developers, an unprecedented opportunity suddenly arose to introduce giant banking under the noses of state and federal legislators. Legislators had repeatedly defeated formal bills introduced by the Bush Administration that would have allowed big banks to cross state lines with impunity. At first, this was hard for me to understand. It only became clear after years of battling government agents who seemed intent upon driving me out of business for no apparent reason.

Led by the political appointees of the Reagan and Bush Administrations, closing banks could eventually create a few mega banks, throughout America, whether or not the states or Congress wanted it. One of these appointees, William Seidman, who set up the RTC, said in 1992 after he retired that interstate banking had already begun—even in states where it was prohibited by state law.

What could not be accomplished with straightforward legislation in Washington or by state legislatures seemed to be happening anyway through a back channel, the Bush S&L clean-up bill.

Federal agencies changed accounting standards that had been used by businesses for decades at banks. Suddenly, perfectly sound, secured business loans, that had been approved by conservative bankers became non-performing. As one Congressman would later say, it was a "shell game" of semantics that allowed regulators to close both insolvent banks and make others appear suddenly short on cash because of new rules.

Lines of credit extended to profitable businesses for decades before the bill was passed, suddenly dried up. Construction loans that are structured with traditional, timed pay-outs as projects neared completion, were suddenly frozen in the middle of construction. Millions of people were thrown out of work all over America. Bankruptcies and unemployment soared while administration officials and the media reported modest gains in bogus economic indicators, like housing starts.

The public, constantly reminded that tax money had bailed out bad banks to the changing tune of $150 billion, $300 billion or $500 billion, could easily believe that the huge number of bankruptcies, failed businesses and other economic problems they were reading about were just the results of more developer greed and bad banking.

The government had changed the rules that had governed who could borrow money and who could not. This was the "credit crunch," a term that was often reported but rarely explained or tied to federal regulators who were closing banks.

One fundamental change involved how much money an individual could borrow. Banks now could no longer lend more than 15% of its capital to any one borrower. This suddenly put many building projects in jeopardy.

Small businessmen who had relied on these lines of credit, construction pay-outs and highly negotiable interest rates on the money they borrowed were no longer on a level playing field. This systematic change in the rules turned a seemingly constructive piece of legislation into a disastrous tool.

By the time the business community understood the new rules, their projects had defaulted, their suppliers would no longer deliver goods or services, forcing many into bankruptcy. That's what happened to our economy—almost overnight. It was a game of dominoes. The first piece was toppled in Washington and pieces of the economy began falling all over the country.

By the early '90's, these new accounting standards became a

runaway train that came crashing headlong into an already stunned U.S. economy.

Under this devious shroud, between 1989 and 1992, the more assets bought or managed by big banks like Chase or Fleet, the larger these banks grew.

If the S&L scandal occurred because of corrupt banking practices and greed in the 1980's, the second banking crisis spawned by the S&L cleanup in the next decade was a systematic bankrupting of America.

It was during the Democratic administration of President Jimmy Carter, that banking deregulation first gained popularity. Congress passed the Depository Institutions Deregulation and Monetary Control Act in his term.

That single measure regulated the rates that banks could pay; credit card issuing savings and loan associations, consumer loans and real estate acquisitions, and development. It also allowed mutual savings banks to make commercial, corporate and business loans and to accept demand deposits in connection with commercial, business, and corporate loan relationships.

However, the most significant thing accomplished under this one bill was raising the federal deposit insurance from $40,000 per account to $100,000. Savings accounts in the U.S. average about $9,000.

When President Ronald Reagan moved to the White House, deregulation became the law of the land. Commercial real estate became even more attractive to investors when Congress also passed the Economic Recovery Act of 1981. This measure allowed increased tax write-off provisions for owning real estate.

Money poured into real estate development projects. These deals were based more on perceived potential tax benefits than on the value of the projects. Deregulation and the tax bill raised real estate speculation to new heights.

It created a sweet opportunity for investors, as well. Securities brokerage firms set up boiler room operations that cleverly moved individuals' investment money in and out of high dividend money market funds, and mutual and pension funds. They also pumped billions of dollars into government insured jumbo certificates of deposit, issued by banks around the country. To earn small interest gains, these operations moved investor money like water from one institution to another, always keeping each investor's exposure under the $100,000 limit. Players in the stock market are the people who benefited from the inflated FDIC insurance, not the average depositor.

This created a hostile environment for banks everywhere. In order to attract deposits, banks upped the ante by offering higher interest on deposits than their competitors. Non-performing loans prevented growth in cash flow. Banks began to flounder. At the same time, investors who had insured deposits at troubled institutions were taking out their interest in cash every month.

"The institutions then had to use other cash deposits to make the interest payments and raised the interest rates they paid out even further to attract the desperately needed cash. The difference between ordinary rates and this inflated interest became known as 'The Texas Premium'," said Texas banker Ed Speed.

In just a few short years, however, the economy reached the boiling point, then burned out. To put it in the simplest terms possible, officers of savings and loans ran up huge losses in bad loans. At the same time, they were paying out unprecedented, high interest rates on deposits. It became a pyramid scheme that began to collapse by the end of the decade.

By the late 1980's, the FDIC, said S&L's had nearly $61 billion in non-performing loans.

Estimates for bailing out failed S&L institutions ranged from a modest $150 billion, up to $500 billion, depending upon whose figures you believed. Lawmakers in Washington were primed to enact strong legislation aimed at making sure taxpayer bailouts of banks would never happen again.

In Washington, debate raged over how to heal the nation's banks. On the floor of both the House of Representatives and the U.S. Senate, drafts of numerous bills to shore up our lending institutions made the rounds between 1988 and 1992.

As the effects of the coming recession began to take hold in every corner of the country, few connected the rising unemployment rate, soaring numbers of business failures and personal bankruptcies to the actions of the government regulators.

However, it soon became clear to some bankers and businessmen that their problems stemmed from more than a cyclical "down turn" in the economy. The actions of the RTC soon became the topic of power lunches in the regions where the agency was active.

It was more than mere coincidence that the financial troubles I was about to face with banks in Connecticut had become legends among businessmen in San Antonio and Houston, Texas. It was more than a cycle that hurled builders, masons, plumbers, developers, and homeowners into bankruptcies all over the country. The one common denominator all these people shared was the single fact that the RTC had shut down their bank or large numbers of banks in their communities. Loans and lines of credit, even for highly profitable businesses with no history of bad debts, dried up.

In my attempt to save my business, I began an investigation that led me to a swarm of federal regulators and the banks they took over.

Once my loan had been targeted by FDIC and RTC regulators, trying to secure a line of credit became almost impossible.

Small banks, even those that were well run, began bleeding from the pressure exerted of regulators who descended upon them.

In May of 1992, ironically, the FDIC asked nearly 300 bankers to write their complaints down. A common complaint was the flood of paperwork that came from the regulators.

Joseph Wachtel, of Big Prairie, Idaho, and president of the $10 million Monitor Bank said regulators sent him forty letters in just three months explaining new or revised banking rules. "That equates to a letter for each day and a half we're open."

BankAmerica Corp., the country's second largest banking company said it had to contend with 200,000 pages of operating rules. And the bank's general counsel, Michael Halloran, said, "Approximately 4,000 pages are added or deleted each month."

The American Bankers Association responded to the FDIC's request, writing that banks now spend between $500 million and $1 billion annually to make sure their regulations are being followed. "The task takes up the time of 75,000 workers," they reported. Luther Thompson, president of the Bank of Atchison County, said directors of that bank were so fed up with compliance they were selling the 122-year-old Rock Port, Missouri bank.

The Congress stepped in again in November of 1991, passing yet another confusing piece of legislation. This piece was called the Federal Deposit Insurance Corp. Improvement Act. If banks were having a difficult time keeping up with the regulators before, this new act added more confusion.

About the same time, President Bush told banks to loosen up on lending while the new law was a signal to regulators to come down even harder on bankers.

The new law was a weak piece of compromise legislation that side-stepped controversial changes in interstate branching and insurance underwriting and securities underwriting by banks. One FDIC official said that law was another "massive piece of banking and regulatory law." Paul Fritts, executive director of the FDIC's Office of Supervision and resolution said "it's not a narrow bill by any means."

Susan Krause, senior deputy comptroller of the currency, told a meeting of the Independent Bankers Association of America held in Texas several months later that the rules surrounding the new legislation were so complex, the government had to establish more than seventy interagency groups to enforce them. Her agency which supervises national banks, planned to add 600 new bank examiners in two years. By January, 1992 the FDIC had shut down hundreds of banks and savings and loan institutions between 1989 and 1991, according to the Office of Thrift Supervision. Two of my banks were among them.

8

DOMINOES

Nowhere were the activities of the FDIC and the RTC felt more than in the building trades and small businesses. While banks appeared to be doing business, the mere threat of being taken over by these agencies had a chilling effect on lending and credit.

While it became widely known in the early 1990s that the country was experiencing a severe "credit crunch," this phenomenon wasn't linked to the actions of these two agencies until the Bush Administration itself stepped into the fray.

"Burned by bad loans and hamstrung by cautious regulators, banks aren't lending the way they used to," USA Today said in an October, 1991 story. An indication that the problem could be laid directly on the door steps of federal regulators, came from the White House that fall when President Bush unveiled plans to "jump start" the economy by encouraging regulators to "ease up" and allow banks to appeal regulatory decisions.

In an interview, Deputy Secretary of the Treasury John Robson was credited with crafting the new Bush plan. He said it was necessary after it became clear that "reasonable credits that would have been extended in normal times" were not available. "And I'm not talking about the go-go credits and the goofy over extensions that were done in the last decade." "It's very clear to me that there are not many character loans made now," Robson said in a frank question and answer interview with USA Today reporter Paul Wiseman. "And the United States of America is going to be a poorer place if there are no more character loans, people betting on people," he said.

"One of the reasons is the ... regulatory influence ... The specter of the S&L collapse haunts (bank and savings and loan) regulators and pushes them in the direction of a never-again mentality, one that leads them more into rigidity and hardness rather than balance and good sense," Robson said. "Regulation isn't a science, it's an art. And it's not a cookie-cutter kind of mentality that brings the most responsible and effective regulation."

In a 1991 report, Congressional Research Service housing specialist Barbara Miles and William Jackson, a specialist in the Money and Banking Economics Division, took a closer look at the problem.

Specifically, they investigated claims that reluctance to lend was damaging the building trades. "Such a visible aspect of the recessionary "credit crunch" is often attributed to collapses of thrift institutions and regulatory dislike of speculative lending to builders," Miles and Jackson said. If bank closings were affecting builders, it was clear that Miles and Jackson attributed any losses directly to a statement made in February, 1990 by Robert L. Clarke, the OCC head who had warned national banks about real estate lending, often blamed for the S&L crisis. Clarke said there had been deficiencies in underwriting, appraisals and loan documentation procedures. He said federal regulators would "take aggressive action on realty loans."

A related story in Institutional Investor the following spring illustrated what Clarke meant to do.

"As real estate values throughout New England melted like snow in a premature thaw, a posse of OCC examiners descended on the region," the newspaper said. "Millions of dollars' worth of once acceptable loans—such as the kind under which a developer can't rent all his space but is still making interest payments—were declared non-performing," forcing the banks to post extra (cash) reserves. Like so many tumbling dominoes, cash-short banks cut their dividends, credit-rating agencies cut their ratings, and many bankers, figuring that Washington was telling them not to make so many loans, shut off the cash spigot that helped fuel the region's growth."

A month earlier, regulators were told to ease up by Bush, but the damage had already been done.

In their report to Congress, Miles and Jackson said it was difficult to determine the full effect of closing savings and loans had had on builders. "Unfortunately, analysis is necessarily tentative at this point and few hard data useful in formulating policy are available."

But, they said two things were clear.

"First, thrift failures per se have had relatively little effect on the building industry, although there are some clearly adverse exceptions," they said.

"Second, changes in the regulatory environment stemming from FIRREA and new risk-based bank and thrift capital requirements have had effects ranging from temporary disruptions to apparent lending retrenchments—including the commercial banking system." In other words, closing banks did not in itself cause problems for builders until the agencies that forced the closing became directly involved in the day-to-day operations of the banks they seized.

"It was in the resolution process," Miles and Jackson said, "that most businesses encountered problems."

"In this case, a builder who has an outstanding loan or line of credit may find it conveyed to a new institution which has lending policies very different from those of the original," they said. "The builder may have to scramble to meet new terms or obtain fresh financing. This can be particularly disruptive where a construction project is underway and the builder is making regular draws against the committed financing to complete the project.

"The cases which have resulted in genuine 'horror' stories appear to be those where the 'new lender' is the government regulator—in the case of failed thrifts, RTC. The same stories have arisen when FDIC has been appointed the conservator for failed banks," they noted. The FDIC essentially ran the RTC.

"A builder's loans find their way into RTC's inventory of loans either because the RTC paid off the failed thrift's depositors and took over all the assets directly, or because an acquiring institution refused" to accept the loan and turned it back to the RTC. "In such cases, a builder who may have counted on a rollover or refinancing could find loans called due instead, and outstanding credit lines canceled. There have been cases reported of builders whose loan draws were delayed without warning or explanation, forcing a slowdown in construction, which then resulted in loss of sales. This then led to RTC reappraisals based on the lost sales, which led to reductions in the construction loan and a cash squeeze which forced builders to stop work altogether. Since the draws were needed to pay for work already done or materials already delivered, liens would be placed on the project by unpaid subcontractors and suppliers," Miles and Jackson said in a May

1991 report to the Congress.

The overall lending climate, they said, created a perverse situation that further jeopardized borrowers—particularly people who had always paid their bills.

"Where lenders must retrench, they are more likely to call in the good loans than the bad loans, simply because there is a higher probability of actually being paid," the congressional researchers said.

9

HOUSING STARTS

Richard Trauner decided to develop twenty-two acres of land in Fishkill, a small town in upstate New York. He made the decision to build there because his bank had enthusiastically courted the prospect of making a profit on 156 townhouses he planned to build and sell just before the bank bailout began.

Key Bank in Southeast, New York was anxious to do business, Trauner said. The bank had agreed to finance the land purchase as long as Trauner and his partner also took out a construction loan with the bank. They agreed.

After wading through three years of bureaucratic hassles the project was about to move forward when the bank suddenly tried to back out of the deal. Trauner said the bank no longer wanted to lend.

The bank could not be reached for comment.

"There was no one else we could get the construction money from," Trauner said. "They didn't want to give us the money because they wanted out of the real estate business.

The bank reluctantly made the deal and the construction began. Units went on sale in August of 1990. Despite the fact that the project was under construction, thirty-nine of the forty-four units in the first phase of the project were sold by October.

Although the town houses were selling at a brisk pace, Trauner said the bank continued to balk.

"We had sales, we had contracts and mortgage approvals," he said, but unidentified officials at the bank suddenly refused to advance further funds needed to complete the project.

"We needed an extra $200,000. We asked them and at that point we had twelve closings scheduled for January and February," he said. Those sales were never closed.

"They were going to be getting back a minimum of $100,000 per unit or $1.2 million over the next two months anyway," the developer said. "It was clear the bank was going to be paid off," but their attitude was 'we want out,'" Trauner said.

"I tried to get a hold of the president of the bank no less than fifty times," Trauner said. "This is a fellow I know and dealt with. He would not take my calls. Finally I caught him by accident. I had his private number and he answered it himself after hours."

According to Trauner, the president said he'd try to get the payout approved, "but I never heard from him again. He would not talk to me."

Through a series of maneuvers only explained from Trauner's point of view, he said the bank moved against him legally and eventually forced him to abandon the project. "They kept the builder and continued the project."

About two years later, he said, the bank resold the same properties.

"I was forced out and had to turn my corporate stock in to the bank. The builder was a partner and I don't believe that he owns any more stock in it either. The bank actually owns the project, but they are using him to continue the project," said Trauner, who called this episode "one of the wildest stories in the country."

"It was probably the only successful project in the northeast at the time because the real estate market had bottomed out."

"It was literally the hottest project going but they refused to let us advertise. They wouldn't give us any money for advertising. When they cut you off, that's what they do.

"They put this loan in special assets in their work-out group and took it out of their regular loan portfolio," he said. Although the loan was not delinquent, Trauner said they treated it as a loan default.

"They just wanted us out because we had money coming to us. It was the most unbelievable situation I've ever encountered. They were monitoring us and they knew what was going on and they prevented us from finishing and people (prospective buyers) were backing out left and right."

Across the border in Connecticut, Tony DaCunha owned The Craftsman Land Development, a Danbury company he started in 1981 to build houses and develop land into building lots.

"I don't want to come across as being bitter, because we lived very well," said DaCunha when we initially asked him to tell his story. DaCunha's company projects failed, and he says it was the federal government that drove him under. His projects had to compete with those the RTC had seized from competing companies. When the Feds discounted the property they held, his company could no longer survive in a tight market.

Although DaCunha did not know Trauner, their difficulties occurred at about the same time federal regulators had swarmed through the northeast closing banks and seizing assets.

"It really seemed that once the FDIC started to close banks, property was depreciating. They kept pushing property (values) down and it reached a point where there was no equity left and no market to purchase properties we were building," he said.

"This is partly due to the fact that the government agencies were dumping their property that they had already foreclosed on at other banks. They dump it under the pretense of getting back as much taxpayer money as possible, so they can just dump it. You can't compete. And, this produces a psychological effect on prospective buyers who wait to see how low prices can go.

"That's why our business failed. We do not have a cash flow in land development or construction. You do not have a daily or weekly cash flow. You primarily survive on sales," he said.

Like many builders, DaCunha's company used a credit line to build projects. The FDIC stepped in and began giving orders at his bank while Craftsman Land Development was in the middle of a building project like Trauner's.

"At the time we had about $300,000 left to draw. The project was in the 85 percent range of completion, and ironically, the day we were supposed to pick up a check for about $80,000, the bank closed at 12 o'clock. We were not able to pick up the check." At the same time they learned that the company could no longer draw on its line of credit either.

"We were out of funds," DaCunha added with some excitement. "We couldn't pay the subcontractors that had just finished working. They have no more funds to finish the project but they still send you the monthly bills for interest. What does that do? It puts that project into a tailspin," he said.

Overnight, the Craftsman Land Development Corporation was headed for bankruptcy.

"In most institutions where the FDIC took over, the people we had previously dealt with from the bank were removed," DaCunha said. "Then you have a lag period of up to three to four months before you have a person to speak to about your loans or the credit lines already approved for your project. By the time an officer is put in charge of your loan again, everything you've built is just eroding," he said.

"You realize that they are just going to dump your project on the market. And they are going to come after you for the deficiency judgment (the difference between discount sales and what the contractor owes.) Your hands are tied. There is no mechanism to bring the creditor, which was us, and the lenders or the government into a forum where we could come up with an equitable solution," DaCunha said.

"I have a gut feeling that the RTC and the FDIC are really more concerned about perceptions from journalists than they are going to be in resolving the issue equitably for the taxpayer. I have seen too many projects that would have been more profitable if they had allowed the present owner or builder to complete the project. The taxpayer would have been better off," DaCunha said.

In an attempt to save another project, DaCunha said he once tried to work out a rental arrangement with the FDIC but that also failed.

"I wanted to rent the project. There would be no profit but the cash flow would carry the debt service so the taxpayers' loan would be covered. It could not happen. I mean, there is no mechanism," he said. "I had to understand the RTC was only created in 1989 and they were not prepared to be logical at all. They are still filtering out who is going to be in charge," he said.

"The ironic part is that I have been through five different individuals from the FDIC since 1990. Projects are unique. There are demographics, regional considerations, values they are not prepared to deal with", DaCunha said, "because they have their rules. Some days you make headway, but then there are too many levels to work through. You can't be too creative. It's frustrating."

DaCunha said an RTC rule further complicates workouts. People who have been in the business for twenty or twenty-five years are not allowed to be employed by the RTC or the FDIC.

"With our experiences, we can't go back in and assist if we owe money." He said job application forms say that persons who owe more than $50,000 to any institution cannot apply.

"So, they get inexperienced people who basically sound like collection agencies.

"A lot of us are just waiting for the judgments to pile up. Growth cannot happen. There's no money out there being circulated. Without it, no expansion can take place," DaCunha said.

10

No Sale

In a depressed real estate market like that experienced in most parts of Maine in 1991, you'd think Jackie and Alvin Brown would have felt privileged. Their house not only sold while the homes around their small 20 acre farm sat idle that year, it was nearly sold twice—to the same buyer.

The Browns owned twenty acres of fenced-in fields, a brook, a 2,500 square foot bow house and a three story barn with running water. But the Browns were forced to sell their home in an attempt to avoid foreclosure after they filed bankruptcy in June that year. Although this working farm had been appraised at nearly $400,000, they accepted a low bid of $275,000 from an anxious buyer. "The bank that was holding liens against the property refused to accept our buyers contract," Jackie said. So a house that could have been sold for $275,000 went on the auction block instead.

That deal was quashed by a set of still fuzzy and mysterious circumstances. Their bank, Maine National, was in trouble and began calling in loans, even those held by long-standing, reliable customers like the Browns. The bank was owned by the larger

Bank of New England, which was also under siege and eventually sold to Fleet Bank of Rhode Island. The Browns' demise was also engineered by federal regulators who really pulled the strings at their bank.

The second time, the buyer who had repeatedly tried to get Maine National to accept his $275,000 contract, bid on the house again at auction. Eventually he bought the property through the Feds for $175,000 or $100,000 less than his original offer.

"The extra $100,000 was equal to a credit line we owed the bank," Jackie said. "They just wouldn't take the $275,000 he offered." For 49-year-old Jackie and her husband, it was this kind of bungling at the hands of federal regulators that drove their $4 million real estate and development company into the ground.

The Browns lost their home, the construction business they built and other assets when Maine National first came under new federal rules. Despite their mounting troubles, Jackie wryly points out that she did not lose everything.

When everything had been sold, taken or auctioned, Alvin found work at an optical company in a nearby town, and Jackie sold houses for a living. And they got to keep their battered 1987 Subaru station wagon with 64,000 miles on it. This was an unexpected blessing bestowed upon them in an eleventh hour bankruptcy proceeding. The car became the symbol of one small victory in a very nasty war that first began inside the offices of Maine National Bank where she and her husband had always been welcomed customers until 1991.

Coincidentally, the bank itself began to experience auditing difficulties. Federal regulators moved in and began shuffling through loan portfolios. The Browns' up to date but still outstanding loans were reclassified as non-performing loans.

The Feds called $4 million in loans that had been extended to this couple over the years for on-going projects. The Browns, who had always maintained impeccable credit, were stunned when they were told to pay up.

By the time they were facing a court-appointed bankruptcy trustee, the Browns had already been defeated in a war with an elusive and deceptive enemy : a federal agency that many Americans believed was just a government insurer of deposits. In the press, the agency had wrongly been characterized as the benevolent protector of America's savings, not a vehicle for taking it.

Behind the facade of FDIC protection, however, the bank was firmly in the grip of a regulatory agency armed with new rules almost no one understood, including the Browns. Systematically, the bank began to chip away at the couple's holdings.

By almost any reckoning, Jackie and Alvin were what you might call stereotypical Down Easterners. I first met Alvin when I decided to build a modest vacation house in York, Maine. The first time we met, the most striking thing about Alvin was his long, snowy white beard which reminded me of Santa Claus. That became my nickname for him.

Alvin and Jackie built a business, one house at a time. By vocation, Alvin was an industrial arts teacher in the 1970's; a hammer and nails kind of guy who knew what it was like to work with his hands. Their farm wasn't some Yuppie enclave either. During school vacations, Alvin built houses to earn a living between semesters.

"There really weren't any jobs he could do summers," Jackie recalled, "so we started this business." Initially, they built single family houses like mine on the Maine coast. In the first year, they had built and sold eight homes, something that attracted the attention of officials at Maine National.

"We had a lot of unsecured debt out there," Jackie said, talking about loans granted to them without collateral. "We had done a lot of business with the same bank for a long time. There was a lot of depth to the relationship" she said in a long, rambling interview.

"We had people calling us, asking do you need a credit line?" We took them because we thought we needed the money to complete our projects in hard times."

The business grew and they branched out into commercial development as well as residential building.

They made frequent visits to their banks and during one of those trips, Alvin mentioned wanting to buy a piece of land a real estate broker had offered to sell him. A deal was worked out where the bank would give him a separate advance to buy the land. When a maze of necessary zoning approvals were issued, the bank said it would give the Browns another construction loan.

In Maine, as elsewhere in the country, this was how developers were able to mount one project after another. It was a routine way of doing business and it was how the Browns rolled their small, "mom and pop" home building business into a million dollar enterprise in just a few years.

But things changed suddenly when the bankers they had known for years began asking for additional signatures, appraisals and other things that had never been required in the past for good bank customers.

One of the things Alvin signed was something known as a "cross collateral" loan. Unbeknownst to the Browns, it would become the instrument that would undo them. Business in Maine was still based on your word, not what you signed or didn't sign. "They respect you here for who you are and relied on your reputation," Jackie said.

But odd things began to happen.

The bank called Alvin in and asked him to tie some outstanding, but up-to-date loans to their home mortgage. If he refused, the bank told him, they could not continue to give him the lines of credit they had promised. Alvin signed.

Next, two seemingly qualified buyers for homes Alvin had built could not get mortgages at the bank. This was a puzzling decision made by a bank that had loaned Alvin the money to build those same houses. By granting those mortgages, the bank would have spread out its risks and Alvin could have paid off his loan to them immediately after the closing. The buyers had been qualified by this bank's own criteria, according to Jackie. It was a queer decision for a bank to stand in the way of this kind of transaction since it would have eliminated the Browns' debt to them.

When the Browns began to experience financial difficulties, they thought they could survive as they had in earlier recessions. It would not be so easy this time.

In neighboring New Hampshire, federal regulators were closing banking institutions at such an alarming rate, Gov. Judd Gregg made an urgent appeal to Washington to halt it.

"Worried about the spiraling costs of bank failures, officials in New Hampshire and neighboring states have persuaded regulators to stop lowering the boom on troubled institutions," one financial story reported. Gregg asked Federal Deposit Insurance Corporation officials to "inject money into the state's shakiest banks rather than shut them down," the story said. Then it outlined a prescription laid out by Gregg to stop the glut of closings.

The FDIC could guarantee bad loans, put in capital, then seek buyers for the institution. It became known as the "Open Bank Resolution" and was drafted to stave off panic by allowing banks to keep operating while buyers of failing institutions were sought. In addition, it was supposed to enable the FDIC to avoid dumping assets like the Brown's $400,000 house for $175,000. While

Gregg's plan made sense in New Hampshire, the FDIC was under enormous pressure to do it's job—close banks deemed insolvent and liquidate its assets as quickly as possible.

An FDIC insider told me that regulators had already dismantled as many banks as possible in New Hampshire by the time the "Open Bank Resolution" got a hearing. The financial climate in Connecticut where I did business was no better. As bank closings mounted, loans were drying up all along the eastern seaboard for reasons borrowers could not immediately discern.

But the bankers and some business organizations knew all too well what was happening. They also knew what these deliberate closings would do to the economy although few people outside of these industries made the connection at the time or even years afterward. It was a clumsy, hazardous handling with a penetrating resonance.

"I would call it a credit catastrophe rather than a crisis," said Peter Gioia, head of research at the Connecticut Business and Industry Association, talking to the Hartford Courant. "Banking in Connecticut is changed forever," he said in the fall of 1991, four months after Jackie and Alvin had filed bankruptcy in Maine.

The catastrophe Gioia referred to concerned the swiftness and rate at which banks in that state were being closed by the FDIC. In ten months, about 16 commercial banks in Connecticut with assets totaling more than $12 billion were seized by federal regulators. State Banking Commissioner Ralph Shulansky said at least that many Connecticut banks would be seized and closed the following year.

"There's going to be a lot of economic bloodshed," Shulansky told construction professionals at a meeting that autumn.

Yes, one of them agreed, and, "we have a lot of babies being thrown out with the bath water," said architect David N. LaBau.

But this fiscal siege they all referred to had begun at least a year earlier in the northeast and had already devastated Texas and other western states.

Mary-Liz Meany, a spokesperson for the American Banker's Association saw how fast the Feds were taking over banks as early as May of 1990.

"It used to take a whole weekend to shut down a bank," she said. "Now, the Federal team of regulators generally goes in on Thursday armed with computers, works furiously through the night and reopens the bank under new management on Friday with no interruption in service."

For most of their twenty years in business, the Browns had never missed a loan or mortgage payment. But when the Maine economy slipped and their bank no longer lent home-buyers money, their loans began to fall behind. Without warning, the bank began to surround them. First they confiscated all the money they had in checking, savings and payroll accounts. Next, they demanded full payment for all outstanding loans and lines of credit. The Browns didn't know what had hit them.

"The regulators were in and out of those banks on a daily basis," Jackie learned. "The banks were scared. No one seemed able to tell us why they called everything. That's what ruined us. I feel like everybody is looking at us, looking at us like we did something wrong. We didn't. We always paid our bills and paid on time." Yet the bank foreclosed on their home.

"We reminded them that we were current on our home mortgage payment," Alvin said. "They reminded me that I had signed those cross collateral agreements which meant they could seize all of my assets to settle the outstanding loans, Alvin said, "I signed those notes with people I trusted and had done business with for years. I never expected them to go after us the way they did."

"When the FDIC stepped in after the audits and shredding of loans, it was apparent they were not interested in making any deal," Jackie said. "They did not care what kind of past relationship we had with those bankers. We knew we were all done. We filed (bankruptcy), but were forced to do it. I was taught that people believe in trust, ability and reputation. To them, we became just numbers. No one gave a [illegible]."

So, when Jackie stood before Bankruptcy Court Trustee William Hallison, she didn't expect to be treated fairly. Their final appearance, after all, was now just a formality.

"This woman now makes her living selling real estate," her lawyer said at the meeting. "She needs this vehicle to show houses and needs the car to continue making a living."

The trustee who had studiously avoided making eye contact, raised his head slowly from the files on his desk. He nodded, affirming what the lawyer had just said. Jackie Brown could keep her five year old car.

It was a final, unexpected act of decency in proceedings that had been anything but decent—especially in Maine where decency and common courtesy had always been one of the unwritten, unsigned agreements required of residents.

11

EVICTIONS

The RTC had also become the largest landlord in the country in less than threeo years. Nationwide, some said, they routinely evicted low income families illegally.

Kathy Brown, who works with a non-profit, community based organization in East Boston called City Life said she began to hear about RTC evictions early in 1991.

"My understanding of the RTC's eviction policy was that it wasn't just a Massachusetts policy, it was a U.S. policy," she said.

City Life joined together with approximately twenty other non-profit agencies in an attempt to stop a wave of moves against low income families occupying RTC-managed buildings.

When City Life first began contacting tenants at foreclosed properties taken over by the RTC, they often found those buildings already vacated.

"Given how many stories we've heard of people being told to leave, it's a good assumption that a lot of people are told to go. When somebody tells you to leave, a lot of people think they have to," she said. "In a community where we work with a large percentage of people that are Latino, they are less aware of their rights because of language," Brown said.

The low income families living in these RTC held buildings in East Boston often had to contend with what some community groups said were unsafe, unsanitary conditions.

In the summer of 1991, housing activists like Kathy Brown called Democratic Congressman Joseph P. Kennedy, whose office investigated and confirmed many of the stories they had heard about the often cruel handling of tenants in the buildings they managed.

In a letter fired off to Secretary of Housing and Urban Development Jack Kemp, Kennedy said he wanted Kemp to come down on the RTC and come down quickly. Kemp and Kennedy, apparently became allies in this attempt although Kemp's role was not immediately known.

"With more than 70,000 properties under its control, the Resolution Trust Corporation is now the largest landlord in the United States, Kennedy said in a letter to Kemp. "It has come to my attention that in some areas of Massachusetts, the RTC and it's agents have been illegally evicting low-income tenants, failing to maintain properties in habitable conditions and ignoring state and local landlord/tenant laws," the congressman said. "The RTC's own policy ... prohibits them from evicting tenants" whose incomes fall below the area's median income.

Kennedy called the agency's actions "high-handed and irresponsible, then cited examples to make his point. "In East Boston, the RTC is landlord in at least six occupied multi-family buildings. Families in these buildings suffer problems ranging from unsafe physical conditions, to illegal rents in excess of those permitted by rent control, and threats of illegal evictions all at the hands of RTC's agents," Kennedy said.

"In one case, the agency brought all the tenants to court for a mass eviction for no reason other than to take possession of the building. All of these tenants were living in deplorable conditions, paying illegally high rents and all were low income," he said.

"The RTC has strong-armed tenants at one building into leaving their homes without the benefit of a court hearing," which is illegal in Massachusetts, said Kennedy. "Local real estate agents and bank personnel from Colonial Savings Bank have told Latino immigrant tenants they would all have to move. One family, against their will and desire, did leave. The other four families were relieved to learn from a local agency, the East Boston Ecumenical Community Council, that they would not have to move.

"Tenants at another building over-heard hired real estate agents and Colonial Savings Bank personnel outside of their buildings saying that they would quickly empty the buildings of tenants in rent controlled units," Kennedy said.

Finally, Kennedy told Kemp "The RTC evades Boston's rent control laws, refuses to register these buildings and charges illegally high rents. Tenants in each of these buildings live with lead paint, rodent and insect infestations, lack of security, no smoke detectors, broken doors, windows, and much more," Kennedy said.

As activist Kathy Brown had long suspected, the RTC problems experienced in Massachusetts were part of a wider, national problem.

"Apparently, the situation in East Boston is not unique," the congressman said. "Similar incidents have occurred outside of my district in Dorchester, Haverhill, and other communities" in Massachusetts. "It is my understanding that similar problems, perhaps on a larger scale, have been occurring in New York City, Texas and other locations," the Massachusetts Democrat said.

"When I first learned of one ... incident, my office spoke to RTC officials and thought the matter was resolved," Kennedy said. But, "two months later, the same Boston lawyer was doing the same thing in Dorchester. The RTC must reign in its lawyers, real estate brokers, bank officials and other agents operating under its name," Kennedy said.

"Working families have already been asked to pay too much for the S&L crisis," he said, zeroing in on the real problem these people were facing. It was bigger than a few buildings in Boston, or just a few cities in the state of Massachusetts.

"The absolute last thing the RTC should be doing is illegally evicting low-income families from their homes, adding to the growing problems of displacement and homelessness," Kennedy said. "Low income families, who are already being asked to pay thousands of dollars for a crisis they did not create, will not be victimized again by illegal evictions."

12

THE BUNGLED BAILOUT

These testimonies tell nearly identical stories. Examining the nature of the indiscretionary "hit now, ask questions later" policy of the FDIC and RTC, it is easy to see why the experiences of these banks and borrowers would be the same.

These regulators and agencies wore blinders and cast large nets. A closer look at the agencies structure, shows they were unregulated, monster bureaucracies with control of massive amounts of power and money. Wide open for abuse, as replete with chaos as it was with opportunism, the RTC made a deep impression on our economy even though most of us didn't realize it.

When you factor in what it would cost almost one million individuals driven into bankruptcy by this regulatory onslaught, the costs we heard about from our elected officials in Washington became meaningless and nattering. If you totaled the wholesale losses in real estate values, the number of businesses that went bust and the number of jobs that disappeared, the real costs were higher than anyone could honestly measure.

Fueled by the knowledge that no matter who they lent money to, the Federal Government would insure depositor's funds, as banks across the United States went on a lending spree during the "go-go" years of the 1980's. Many claimed that the excesses of the 1980's would lead to a correcting period, but no one could have imagined the blind excess of this runaway "correction."

One thing to keep in mind whenever reading any stories about the banking dilemma, whether you are reading about the industry's current sins or past transgressions, banks have been heavily regulated for the past sixty years.

"Congress and the previous (Reagan) administration created the savings and loan debacle," said William H. Rivoir, Arizona's former superintendent of banks in testimony that was eventually read into the Congressional Record in the fall of 1991.

This commonly known fact was rarely mentioned in a flurry of stories that came out once banks began to fail in large numbers in the late 1980s. This crisis didn't just happen. It was the creation of legislation, lax enforcement of regulations that were on the books, but it was characterized as this Nothing that was having an immeasurable effect on our lives. That was fiction.

Even earlier in the last decade under deregulation, a wide variety of federal agencies were charged with monitoring our banking systems and its practices. Bank deregulation did not free banks to operate outside of the keen eye of government auditors.

In 1992, a Ralph Nader watchdog organization leveled attacks aimed at both the Congress and the auditing agencies charged with monitoring banks.

"To date, the Congress has failed to represent the American people when it comes to the S&L bailout," they said in a 44 page report called "Beyond The Botched Bailout."

"First, Congress—along with the deregulatory zealots in the Reagan administration—simultaneously decontrolled the thrifts, pulled the regulatory cops off the banking beat, and expanded taxpayer exposure to the eventual costs. Now, every single time the Bush Administration has asked for new funds for the S&L bailout, Congress has essentially rubber stamped the request," authors Sherry Ettleson and Patrick Woodall said.

The point they make certainly adds clarity to what had seemed a complicated story about a crisis that just appeared out of nowhere. Certainly, it was no accident that whatever sins banks committed, they were usually carried out within full view of government agencies charged with watching our finances. By law, banks are supposed to be examined annually. Depending on whether an institution is classified as a state bank, a federal bank or a bank holding company, as many as four separate government agencies might have had access to their books. Why none of these agencies ever detected or reported these widespread abuses remains one of the mysteries of this national crisis.

When the savings and loan story began to surface in the late 1980's, it was portrayed as a soiree created solely by unscrupulous bankers who bought luxury homes, cars and vacations with depositor and stockholder funds. It was as if these banks had been operating in some off-shore facility in the Caribbean or from hotel rooms in Switzerland.

When the boom fell, the same regulatory agencies charged with watching banks in the first place were then ordered by the Congress to help clean up a fiscal mess they said the banks alone had created.

The government has always played a role in this scenario. "The owners and operators of troubled" banks "had nothing to lose by engaging in riskier lending—but had much to gain if such lending brought big earnings and returned the institutions to solvency," congressional researchers have said in reports widely available in Washington. "The government, through its policy of forbearance, did not act to constrain risky lending, even though it did stand to lose from such lending practices. Thus, all the incentives worked to encourage risky lending on the part of troubled institutions. This practice generated further losses."

By late 1989, banks everywhere were in trouble. The Congress maintained a revolving list of 1,000 troubled banks out of 13,000. The list was kept secret.

"The failures precipitating the cleanup and their great expense were due to three interrelated phenomena," Congressional Research Service analysts Barbara Miles and Thomas Woodward said in a 1991 report. First, they said, "the maturity risk—borrowing short term deposits to lend for long-term mortgages" weakened savings and loans. "Second, the presence of federal deposit insurance ... removed any incentive for depositor concern over the safety and soundness of individual institutions." Finally, a widespread policy among regulators "allowed failing institutions to continue to operate long after they would have gone out of business except for the federal deposit guarantees." In other words, banks that began to bleed financially were repeatedly bailed out by the FDIC, long before any formal bailout began.

Working in concert with the FDIC, the RTC built a new twelve-story building in Arlington, Virginia. While the Bureau of Labor Statistics was reporting high unemployment throughout the country and other economic indicators were plummeting, there was no shortage of jobs at these two agencies.

In the first two years of RTC existence, the FDIC hired 3,646 new employees, a 45% increase over a similar period. That brought the number of workers to 11,000. In its 1989 annual report, released in 1990, the agency predicted the number of people it would need to run the agency would climb as high as 19,000. Hundreds of regulators were trained at the Virginia headquarters, then sent to regional offices throughout the United States to close banks, turn their assets over to RTC regulators who paid out deposits and liquidated bank assets.

Even in setting up offices, lawmakers said the agency was spending too much money on nonessentials.

In an attempt to boost morale, the agency once bought a dozen golf shirts and 36 coffee mugs with the agency logo embossed on them, according to printed reports. These trinkets cost $3,000.

In another highly publicized incident, Michael Martinelli, the former head of the RTC in Kansas City decorated his office with $26,000 worth of artwork. When this became known, he was quickly reassigned to Washington but kept his $110,500 a year job. The House subcommittee on Financial Institutions Supervision released a report in September, 1991 saying both the FDIC and the RTC were spending thousands of wasted dollars on incidental items. The report said the FDIC had spent more than $177,000 on art for the Arlington headquarters. The office in San Francisco had paid $1,362 for a desk and another $1,126 for a credenza.

But these criticisms were minor compared to other charges leveled at the agency. A number of informed citizens and public officials said that setting up the agency was simply a fatal mistake that would reek havoc on the economy.

"It is now clear that the agency was structured to fail from the beginning," a public interest group said two years after the RTC began closing banks.

While the RTC appeared to be another government agency, in fact, it was a hybrid, quasi-governmental giant that operated somewhere in between the lines of a private company and an arm of the government.

"From the beginning, the politicians who created the RTC

sought to minimize the magnitude of the agency's task. They conceived the agency as a temporary entity, with a short life span, designed to complete a discrete and manageable task," said Sherry Ettleson and Patrick Woodal, an attorney and staff researcher for a consumer advocacy organization in Washington. The RTC's task was monumental and a potential nightmare for the politicians who created it. If this entity did not complete its job swiftly and efficiently, political heads could roll. Therefore, a hybrid was created that bowed to no single master, according to the House Banking Committee Task Force on the RTC.

"Under the law, the RTC is treated as a 'mixed-ownership corporation,'" said Congressman Bruce Vento, a Democrat from Minnesota. "Under this structure, the government pays for its operations but it has a corporate structure with a board of directors" who run the corporation. As such, it is "allowed to avoid all the protections heretofore thought necessary to the prudent operations of a government function," a committee report said.

"The effect of the Financial Institutions Reform, Recovery, and Enforcement Act's (FIRREA) provisions for its structure and operation is almost perverse in that it denies the flexibility that is given to any other government corporation while avoiding the safeguards in management and auditing that necessarily apply to them. FIRREA chose the worst of both government form and business form," Vento said.

In other words, the RTC was not set up as a pure government agency and could therefore operate without the rules of accountability true agencies must follow. If it solved the banking crisis, its creators could say it was their legislation that put banking back on sound footing. If, however, it failed, the blame would fall squarely in the backs of a board of directors, as if the RTC were a private entity. The Congressional Research Service reported that a lack of funding set the RTC up to fail from the beginning.

"The RTC has repeatedly run low on funds, thus impeding the cleanup process. Whenever this happens, the costs go up because the institutions not closed continue to lose money," the analysts said two years after the RTC was formed.

If the RTC had been just another cog in the wheel of governance, it might not have mattered.

"Not since the 1930s has a new agency arisen so quickly and taken on so significant an economic role," Public Citizen's Congress Watch said. The consumer and environmental advocacy group founded by Ralph Nader in 1973 blamed this single act for numerous economic problems throughout the United States.

"Following the 1988 election, the Bush Administration decided it was time to solve the S&L crisis. It quickly prepared legislation, which it sent to Congress in February of 1989, to recapitalize the deposit insurance fund, impose new requirements on thrifts, and, almost incidentally, create the RTC. In its rush to pass legislation, Congress paid little attention to the vast agency it was creating."

Nevertheless, the RTC was formed and told to resolve the situation in one of three ways. A failed bank could be bought by other institutions, another institution could receive the deposits of a failed bank or the RTC could take over the institution, pay depositors off and then sell off its assets.

The RTC was a legislated mess, a dangerous instrument that could create severe economic consequences if used improperly.

In two years, the RTC became an unwieldy giant. It controlled 585 S&Ls with a total of $350 billion in assets. It was expected to acquire an additional $150 billion for a total of $500 billion. No known entity in the world controlled so much, so quickly.

Assets taken over by the RTC included securities like junk

bonds, mortgages and other loans as well as land, houses and commercial buildings. These holdings were the homes and businesses of citizens, although the notes or loans were held by banks the government deemed insolvent. When the corporation was set up, the Congress set in motion a major force that could transfer huge holdings from the current owners to whoever had the funds to buy. The corporation was told to dispose of these properties "in the most timely, least disruptive, most efficient manner possible." This mandate was governmental gibberish.

"There are major marketing, legal, environmental, and other difficulties in disposing of these assets," congressional analysts said. Nevertheless, the RTC had to dispose of these assets rapidly because the corporation, by law, was supposed to go out of business by 1996.

"As the largest corporation in terms of assets and the largest holder of real estate in the United States, the RTC has become a major economic force," Public Citizen's said in it's scathing report released in March of 1992. "With so many assets to sell and so much money to spend, the RTC is having a critical impact on the financial and real estate markets, affecting the lives of every American consumer and taxpayer. Unfortunately, it is undertaking this task in a manner that is both needlessly expensive for taxpayers, and damaging to the economy." The RTC had additional problems in getting rid of assets because they had little idea of what they owned, or what property was sold.

According to Congressman Joseph Kennedy, the Denver and Washington offices each sold the same office building within two days. "There is no computerized sheet of what their assets are. The right hand doesn't know what the left hand is doing. They have simply botched it to no end," he said. Kennedy also became aware of $7 billion that the agency just lost through their Denver office.

"It hired a consulting firm for something like $15 to $20 million to find out what happened to the $7 billion," he said. The money was never located.

By June 31, 1991, the RTC had taken control of 623 institutions and was operating 193 of them. At that time, at least 158 more institutions were about to fall into RTC hands with another 300 to follow. Banks operated by the RTC continued to lose money because of the way they were managed. First, the agency immediately lowered interest rates, a move that automatically sent deposits to other banks. Meanwhile, the RTC had to pay operating losses during the resolution process.

"The costs of delay takes several forms," congressional researchers said. "To prevent outflows of deposits from conservatorships that might drain cash, the RTC must pay higher interest rates than it would otherwise. Further, it must slow the pace of resolutions and thereby incur greater operating costs. If the pace of the cleanup is slowed by reducing the number of institutions placed in RTC hands, it increases the losses that institutions rack up before seizure. Finally, postponement or resolution may influence the bids received for failed institutions, and the way the sales are structured." The administration estimated the costs of delay in May, 1991 ran about $8 million per day.

While funding for the RTC was debated numerous times after it was formed, the law which created the bailout agency required it to solve the banking problem quickly. The Congress had created a schizophrenic monster. While it was supposed to resolve the crisis quickly, and do it with the least impact possible on the economy, the mandate became disasterous.

"The RTC has interpreted this mandate to require it to dispose of its voluminous and diverse portfolio of assets as quickly as possible but at the best price" without affecting the local market, the Nader organization said in its report.

"Members of Congress then confused matters further by urging the RTC to sell its assets at an even faster pace—and by complaining about the low return on assets. Plainly, these instructions can not be followed. These strong incentives to sell fast, combined with the poor condition of the market, has made it impossible to recoup the full value through sales. Ultimately, the taxpayers, who are paying the bailout bill are hurt most by this costly method of disposing of assets," they concluded.

Congressional researchers Miles and Woodward saw the same handwriting on the wall.

"The growing magnitude of this task has already raised questions," they said. "In real economic life" these competing needs "are traded off against one another rather than attained simultaneously."

The magnitude alluded to by these researchers concerned the complexity and varied nature of the many assets the RTC held.

"A wide variety of problems" are involved with "virtually all types of assets except cash and government securities," the Congressional Research Service said in a Library of Congress report in the fall of 1991. "Many securities, for example, are junk bonds which are not currently saleable except at very steep discounts. Discounts are also necessary for low-interest rate loans. Loans which are not current generally have to be restructured to be disposed of, or must be foreclosed."

Many of the assets the agency dealt with were not straightforward transactions. In many instances, liability for a loan was shared among several institutions. This meant the RTC did not always have clear title to a delinquent loan and therefore could not unilaterally restructure it or foreclose. "This can be a severe impediment where a co-holding thrift which is not held by the

RTC does not want to (assume the inevitable) accounting losses on its books."

This becomes especially critical when the assets involve real estate.

"Not only may title not be clear, but fire sale prices to move large numbers of properties quickly could seriously lower property values in nearby locations," researchers said. "Alternatively, holding to appraised values in weak markets guarantees long holding periods and carrying costs which can easily consume two to three percent of the property's value every month it remains unsold."

In an attempt to clear the books as rapidly as possible, the RTC instituted a sliding discount rate on real estate. In other words, the fire sale prices the congressional researchers referred to were more than theory. It was a reality that many said spelled disaster to local property values across the country. "At least one early study indicates that the impact of RTC land and commercial properties sales is less than may have been feared," the congressional researchers said. Another early study by Kerry Vandell and Timothy Riddiough called 'Housing Policy Debate' supported this conclusion.

The Nader organization, however, had another view.

"The RTC's scheduled markdowns destabilized the market," they said. The RTC had a policy similar to some clothing retailers that factored in regularly marked down property prices. If a property remained unsold after the first six months its price was dropped 20 percent. If the property remained unsold another six months, the price was dropped an additional 20 percent. After 18 months the RTC marked it down a final 10 percent. Real estate could be discounted by as much as 50 percent in an 18 month period. An RTC spokesman said in an interview that they were getting a 95% return on all assets sold. This claim complies with its Congressional mandate. Congressman Joseph Kennedy, however, said the value of the assets were remarked down before their sale so that the agency could make this claim. "It's nothing more than a shell-game," he says. "The problem is that any time you raise these issues you are accused of trying to raise the ultimate bill to the taxpayer."

In commercial properties, the impact of price depletion was more measurable since most of these properties were usually occupied. But residential properties were more sensitive to any flooding of the market with discounted properties.

"Local property values may well be adversely affected by a temporary glut in units for sale," the congressional researchers said. "To the extent that values of houses are lowered by RTC marketing, increased mortgage defaults are probable and some amount of neighborhood instability could arise should values remain low for any length of time. Prices of other houses could well be depressed by this procedure," they said, referring to the automatic discounts used throughout the country by RTC regional offices.

"Nonetheless, the pressure is on the RTC to sell its assets quickly," congressional researchers said. But, clearly, the RTC was having difficulties carrying out this part of the cleanup. By the end of June 1991, it had acquired $330 billion in assets. It had disposed of or "resolved" $172 billion but still held another $160 billion. At the same time, observers predicted the agency would ultimately have to "resolve" an estimated total of $500 billion before it was scheduled to go out of business in 1996.

In order to meet that deadline, regulators would have to quicken an already helter-skelter pace. However, a wide variety of problems stemming from the way the agency was structured from

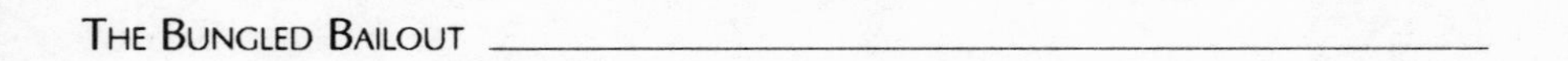

the beginning repeatedly hampered what had become an impossible job.

13

THE GAME

In a rare display of candor, a former Arizona superintendent of banks stepped forward in the summer of 1991 and bluntly told an audience in Phoenix that his state's economy was systematically being destroyed by government bank regulators.

If these charges by William Rivoir had been made at a news conference or in a staff meeting, what he said that day might not have been so explosive. But Rivoir was not speaking into cameras or giving a pep talk to people who worked for him. Rivoir delivered his charge to an advisory board of the Resolution Trust Corporation—the very agency he was criticizing.

And, he gave them a message to take back to Washington. He politely, though clearly, charged the agency with lying by saying they had made "misstatements" about their impact on local economies. Then he warned them to stop.

"I appear before you today in the unenviable position of having to bring you bad news," Rivoir said. "I want you to remember that I am just the messenger. I have personally investigated RTC operations by talking to a wide range of market participants—Realtors, appraisers, investors, developers, syndicators, accountants, and lawyers," he told the board. "It is not my intention to give offense but it will be difficult to avoid, because I have some very direct things to say," said Rivoir, who then launched into a 15-page critique of the agency. It was a chilling litany.

"Contrary to the RTC's public position, loan restructurings are not being pursued, and foreclosure is still the first and only resort," he told them.

"RTC is forcing out of business the very parties who could most effectively assist it in salvaging problem loans and problem projects," said Rivoir. "These people are the real estate professionals who are currently in the deal and are willing to work hard to save it, if only the RTC would take a realistic look at what is left to be saved," he said.

Since Rivoir's statements were eventually read into the Congressional Record, our congressmen and senators could no longer pretend they knew nothing about this runaway agency and the damage it was inflicting.

"RTC personnel are convinced that they have some sort of divine patriotic duty to reek moral retribution on everyone who was ever associated with a savings and loan, even an innocent borrower," Rivoir said. The borrower is rarely mentioned in most stories about the S&L cleanup. "The RTC has developed a paranoia about dealing with anyone who ever had anything to do with a property (they've seized). The RTC Phoenix office has wrongly assumed the role of Lord High Executioner," he said, apparently comparing our federal government with sovereigns of the Spanish Inquisition.

For several years preceding my dealings with this agency, I had seen the fear Rivoir talked about strike grown men dumb. Wherever I went, the names Federal Deposit Insurance Corporation or the Resolution Trust Corporation became interchangeable.

When my troubles first began, I first thought my bankers were the problem. Later I learned it had been the fear of these executioners Rivoir now named in his testimony.

Without warning, businessmen with little or no experience dealing with federal agencies were first confused by a snarl of seemingly endless procedures tied up with their loans. Bankers, fearing their institutions would be summarily closed by the FDIC, complied with the mountains of paperwork borrowers had to sign to continue doing business. Although some like myself and Tony DaCunha had already sorted out most of the pieces in this puzzle by the time we discovered Rivoir's testimony, reading it simply confirmed the mad way in which these agencies were destroying this country—region by region. Whether you were talking to developers, bankers or state officials, one message always seemed to come through—these agencies had the power and clout equal to, if not greater than the Internal Revenue Service. And they scared the hell out of the people who faced them.

Once, when I complained to banking commission officials in Connecticut about RTC attempts to seize my property, they told me their hands were tied. The Feds had illegally placed liens on my property. The Connecticut banking commission told me I would have to appeal to Albany, N.Y. since my bank in Connecticut had been taken over by Chase Manhattan in New York. This was just part of the madness and Rivoir was finally exposing it for the record.

"The actions of the RTC in Arizona are destroying our real estate market, it is shrinking our property tax base, it is hindering the bonding ability of local jurisdictions, and, more to the point, it is causing the RTC to accomplish exactly the opposite of its stated goals, which are to manage the acquisitions of assets from failed savings and loans and to dispose of those assets with the highest possible net recovery for the government and the taxpayer," Rivoir said.

"The situation is so bad that I do not exaggerate when I say that the RTC operations here are illegal, immoral, wasteful and downright stupid," Rivoir said. "Unfortunately, the RTC ... annihilates everyone in its path, pursuing punitive litigation, forcing unnecessary bankruptcies and deliberately destroying the lives and businesses of people whose only sin is that they borrowed from a savings and loan," Rivoir said.

But, he said, the tangle of regulatory paper shuffling in this clean up agency was part of a carefully crafted plan with built-in confusion. Like the banking crisis it was charged with cleaning up, that crisis spawned a second scandal—the RTC itself and the way it did business.

"The RTC's basic design, and virtually all of the policies and procedures that have emanated from it during its relatively short life, have only one true underlying purpose—to shift blame." He said the banking crisis itself was a creation with an ulterior purpose. When it became clear that some one, some government body could be blamed for one of the largest fiscal disasters in American history, the RTC was formed.

"The RTC has reacted to this political reality by creating an enormous bureaucracy that is designed to ensure that it and its personnel never make a decision for which they could be held responsible. There is a policy or a procedure at every step in the process that requires either a mechanical application of a formula or the shifting of the decision to someone outside of the RTC," the commissioner said. "The result has been indecision on so massive a scale that words are inadequate to describe it."

Then Rivoir systematically dissected the agency's operations beginning with how it handles the assets it seizes.

"Asset managers are apparently picked for every reason except competence and knowledge of the local market," he said. "National companies, many of which have highly knowledgeable and competent local offices, can only be listed in the RTC's data base in one location," Rivoir said.

"The RTC's almost total refusal to hire anyone who actually knows anything about the market into which they are to sell assets has become comical," he said. "There have been instances where newly appointed, out-of-town asset managers have come in to take over portfolios of properties in Arizona and have had to ask where the city of Tucson is in relation to Phoenix, or where downtown Phoenix is," he said. "How can these people be knowledgeable enough about our market to manage and sell property here," he asked.

Ironically, Rivoir said, these asset managers are true entrepreneurs in their role as sellers of RTC properties. He said there are no standardized forms for purchases or sales agreements. Brokerage listings, warranty deeds, office building leases, retail leases and other necessary documents are also not standardized. Even worse, Rivoir said, asset managers are charged with "resolving" or liquidating the assets they manage. They are able to do this in a free-wheeling way that ultimately hurts local economies.

This too, Rivoir said, is by design.

"First, it has shifted blame for the failure (to liquidate assets in a timely manner) away from the RTC and onto the asset manager. Second, because of all the reports it requires, it (the RTC) can deflect charges of inaction because it has created a huge paper trail that offers a well documented process as a substitute for real progress."

"When the RTC takes over real estate," Rivoir said, "agency appraisals often aren't worth the paper they're written on because many of its appraisers are unqualified. This, in part, stems from an RTC requirement that appraisal contracts, legal work, property management, sales listings and other jobs go to companies chosen randomly from a list of registered providers. At one bank, Southwest Savings, this random generation process consists of putting slips of paper in a shoe box and picking out names like awarding door prizes." Rivoir said.

"The RTC cannot provide its own appraisers with rent rolls, legal descriptions of the property, a list of recent offers or listing information and offers on similar RTC property," he said. Without these important market factors, Rivoir said, a true appraisal of a property's worth is almost impossible. Therefore, when an appraiser bids on a job, a $2,000 bid could turn out to be a $10,000 job, and the results will be that the appraiser cannot afford to do a good appraisal.

Rivoir's charges were echoed in a damning report by the General Accounting Office (GAO) a year later. Like a sticky web, RTC regulators threw a blanket over assets wherever they went. Almost immediately, real estate values were put in jeopardy. In turn, the value of assets throughout the nation came under this tawdry shroud.

One of the things that made their involvement so comprehensive were the appraisers they hired. The General Accounting Office, an investigative arm of our government, said that most were unqualified. Yet, they could value or devalue large tracts of property through questionable contracts given to them by RTC officials. The RTC had almost no control over who they were hiring, according to the GAO audit of their activities.

In April of 1992, the GAO said an overwhelming 69% of these appraisers were under qualified in education and experience. In a report, the GAO said the RTC managed appraisers poorly and had loose hiring standards. The GAO carefully researched the qualifications of 51 appraisers using data from job applications, resumes, job interviews and other materials submitted by appraisers to the RTC.

The GAO then hired outside consultants to interpret the data, and interviewed former employers, co-workers, and acquaintances of these appraisers.

Noting a 1986 House Government Operations Committee report that had said "faulty and fraudulent real estate appraisals were a serious national problem" costing investors and banks billions of dollars, the GAO questioned why the RTC would not have a specific hiring criteria for a field that already had a questionable reputation.

RTC appraisals are uniquely difficult because the assets they hold are diverse, ranging from single family homes, to office buildings and swamp land. And, they are spread throughout the country where regional markets are widely different," the GAO report said.

Many properties are of poor quality, and the unsettled conditions of the real estate market in 1992 made the assessing even more difficult, the report said. The appraiser had to be familiar with locations, potential and current value, as well as the tax base. RTC guidelines for hiring appraisers, according to the GAO, do not assure this kind of competence.

Of the 51 appraisers that the GAO looked at, only sixteen were deemed qualified. Most failed because they lacked adequate experience in the fields they were assigned to by the agency.

The GAO report also included a rebuttal by RTC officials who said the agency had encountered difficulty hiring appraisers because they needed large numbers of them quickly. While "a few appraisers may have been underqualified," the GAO methodology and requirements had been unfair, the agency said.

According to one appraiser, however, all any person had to do to become eligible to appraise properties held by the RTC was sign on to a master data base until June 1992. The policy was changed then, but Connecticut appraiser, James Boothroyd said the RTC had no initial screening process prior to this time.

"All you had to do was fill out a form and say you can do X, and become part of the RTC's national data base," said Boothroyd. "After that, you got a chance to bid. Only then would they ask for a copy of your resume along with your bid package. But you were already on their list," he said.

When asked for a copy of their qualified appraisers in Connecticut, the RTC sent us a document that listed the appraiser's names, the number of contracts they had been awarded and fees they had been paid.

In one instance, the list said that an appraiser had been given a single contract for $2,500. When contacted, however, that appraiser told us he had actually been given a packet containing 35 separate contracts that totaled more than $80,000. Others who were listed as having one to three contracts said the real number was somewhere between 30 and 50 separate appraisal contracts.

The RTC maintains a "reading room" in Washington where employees field questions related to the agency's asset management. When asked about this contract and fee discrepancy, an unidentified employee said an appraiser may be listed as having only one contract, but may in fact have a "basic ordering agreement" that contains multiple jobs.

When asked why the fees were not totaled, the employee said that the fees were only estimates, "just ball park figures. Don't take the fees seriously. It's the best guess made at the time the data was entered. Its not something we keep a real accurate record of," the

RTC employee said.

Another faulty RTC procedure concerned the use of the real estate broker's opinion on the market worth of property.

"The RTC is paying $3,500 each for simple brokers' opinions on a package of mini-warehouses. Not only is this too much to pay, brokers' opinions are not independent estimates of value," Rivoir said during his lengthy testimony, "they are opinions designed to facilitate a sale, a sale that might not be in the RTC's best interest. Brokers are telling the RTC what they want to hear: that the appraisal is much too high and that the property should be sold for much less. In other words, the brokers want a commission. This is an obvious conflict of interest," Rivoir said, one that seemed widespread throughout the country. The abuses Rivoir exposed did abound.

In Texas, for example, the Ralph Nader organization said a real estate broker reportedly formed the Lung Transplant Foundation in 1991, a medical charity that qualified for the RTC affordable housing program. The program was started to make RTC property available to non-profit organizations like City Life of Boston. The day after the foundation was formed in Texas, it submitted 160 bids for houses. The bids, $500 per house, were almost identical and were submitted by the broker's son. The broker would collect a $500 commission on each for finding a buyer. That's a shell game. The RTC was paying for its own real estate.

Also in 1991, a Boston real estate investment company won the right to buy the CenTrust Tower in Miami, a $170 million building designed by renowned architect I.M. Pei. Winthrop Financial Associates was awarded the sale with a $44 million bid even though the RTC had reportedly received at least three higher bids, including one for $50 million. A principle in Winthrop was reportedly a fraternity brother of T. Timothy Ryan, director of the

Office of Thrift Supervision. The terms of the sale were almost as sweet as the sale itself. Winthrop put up $7.2 million and the remaining $36.8 million was financed by the RTC.

Even after the RTC agrees to sell property, these deals aren't necessarily completed, according to Rivoir.

"The RTC standard purchase form and sales contract is not a contract at all," he said. "It is totally illusory. It specifically states that the RTC has absolutely no duty to live up to its part of the contract. And when the RTC does default, it does so with impunity," the commissioner said. Under the contract, no damages can be assessed against the RTC, regardless of how much damage its actions may have caused," he said, "And don't be misled. The RTC is causing damage."

"The RTC feels no compunction whatsoever about breaking deals in escrow," he said. "This practice is not only reprehensible, it is stupid. Knowledgeable buyers will not put up with this type of practice and they will cease doing business with the RTC."

In another highly questionable practice, RTC bill of sales are also clever devises aimed at distancing the agency from any subsequent legal difficulties, Rivoir says.

"When RTC sells personal property along with realty, it gives a quit claim bill of sale. It sells you personal property, takes your money, and then won't tell you whether it actually owned what it just sold you," he said. "The buyer is completely exposed" to any subsequent legal claims on those items.

If a buyer should be foolish enough to take the RTC on in court, Rivoir said, they're in for a rude awakening.

"The RTC's lawyers have found a perfect client—a client with endless amounts of money who is willing to litigate forever and who exercises no control over its counsel," Rivoir said. "According to its own lawyers, the RTC is endlessly pursuing uncollectable claims, failing to respond to or rejecting reasonable settlement proposals, and pawning off on the lawyers all kinds of non-legal business decisions," he said, making the same charges as Nader's Public Citizen's Congress Watch.

When the Congress created the RTC, Citizen's Congress Watch said they inadvertently created "a public works program for lawyers."

"Unfortunately, the RTC legal program is out of control. Although some of the agency's legal work is done in-house, most is performed by private firms—resulting in staggering costs," the advocacy group said. "The RTC has surpassed the Fortune 500 in its entirety as the nation's largest purchaser of legal services," they said, quoting from various published reports on the agency.

"In 1990, the FDIC and RTC spent $733 million on private lawyers to represent them in civil cases; in 1991, the amount paid out neared $887 million. As of April, 1991, nearly 1,000 law firms or individual lawyers were on the RTC's contractor eligibility list," they said. In one instance, the agency paid the Wall Street firm of Cravath, Swaine and Moore in New York as much as $600 an hour in a junk bond case involving the troubled Drexel Burnham Lambert investment firm.

Rivoir says those attorneys do not always follow the spirit of the law.

"For whatever reason, the RTC hires and apparently, rewards those attorneys who are the most difficult to deal with on a reasonable basis." By way of an example, he cites a case involving construction of the Phoenician Hotel. When the RTC took over this asset, subcontractors who built the hotel filed claims for work they had completed. Instead of negotiating, the case wound up in state court.

"After two years in state court, with trial coming close, the RTC suddenly removed the case to federal court just when state rules would require the RTC to list its witnesses and exhibits," he said. "The subcontractors, who really did do the construction work, and have legitimate claims for payment, have had their claims bought out for a small percentage of their worth, with taxpayer money providing the funds," Rivoir said. "The same taxpayer funds have exhausted those subcontractors by two years of intensive state court litigation. This is done not in the interests of justice or morality, but solely because the RTC has the power to unfairly bludgeon these people with unfavorable settlements," Rivoir said.

Then, in an eloquent, almost sermon—like closing, Rivoir said:

"We find ourselves now with a governmental agency intent, not upon resolving a bad situation in the manner best for all of this country's citizens, but one focused on punishing all of the 'participants' in the S&L disaster, even when those 'participants' were themselves, the victims of the collapse.

"We find ourselves with a governmental agency not striving to construct a long term solution, but one satisfied with viciously attacking each individual problem with no thought for whether that attack forwards the legitimate goals of the RTC.

"And we find ourselves with a government agency whose agents have adopted a rigid moralistic attitude that stifles even rudimentary problem-solving techniques and attitudes," Rivoir said. "Government has a duty to treat its citizens fairly. It must self-police since the powers we necessarily grant government are broad. The RTC has breached this covenant with our citizens, and some measure of control and justice must be restored," he demanded.

"The RTC is violating its own legal mandate by failing to obtain the highest net recovery on assets it is taking back and by causing serious and unnecessary harm to our local real estate market. The RTC is acting in a morally reprehensible fashion by violating its own contracts and wantonly driving individuals and companies into bankruptcy," he charged. "The RTC is wasting millions of dollars of taxpayer money on needless litigation, and it is acting stupidly when it ignores zoning issues, when it refuses to restructure problem assets, when it refuses to ... make any decisions other than default decisions," he said.

One month before Rivoir appeared before this local RTC advisory board, in May of 1991, the RTC National Advisory Board Chairman Phillip F. Searle reportedly had said that he had heard nothing to support claims that the RTC was having a negative impact on real estate markets.

"Tell him that the RTC's activities in Arizona are destroying Arizona's real estate market... Make sure that Mr. Searle cannot make that same misstatement again," Rivoir said.

14

DECEMBER SURPRISE

In the summer before the 1992 November elections, a story surfaced related to a suspected political maneuver by Republicans that was called "The December Surprise."

Simply put, consumer activists, economists and lawmakers suspected the Bush Administration knew the thrift bailout had failed, but planned to keep the lid on the story until after the November elections.

"In December 1992 voters may discover they've been had again," wrote Michael Waldman, director of Nader's Public Citizens Congress Watch in The New Republic Magazine.

"The untold story of this presidential election is how the Bush Administration's bank regulators ... have sought to postpone a commercial banking crisis until after November. Then, soon after the election, the administration will suddenly discover that there is a surprise! a major banking crisis."

Boston College Economist Edward J. Kane concurred, testifying before a House Banking Committee hearing that he believed a "cover up" related to the banking clean up existed.

"The bank insurance fund is following in the same ruts in the same road of forbearance and cover-up that previously led the Federal Savings and Loan Insurance Corporation (FSLIC), the now-defunct S&L insurance fund) to ruin," Kane said. "The understatement of the thrift industry's insolvency's that voters saw in the election of 1988 is closely paralleled by treatment of ... bank insolvencies in the 1992 election," he said.

Robert Litan of the Brookings Institute also saw something ominous, noting that there had been a noticeable slow down in the number of banks closed by government regulators just before the November election. "There is a disturbing pattern to the FDIC bank closure rate," he said. "Something's fishy."

At best, these observations were indications that something had gone wrong with the bailout. But, it would have been a transparent move on the part of the administration to suddenly announce a larger problem than anyone in Washington had previously detected.

While no one doubted the administration might withhold damning information, particularly anything even remotely related to the economy, news that the bank bailout had failed was not news in Washington. In this book we have purposely reprinted just a few of the widely available documents we were able to obtain in just three months of reporting through routine channels. Clearly they show the bailout had floundered from the very beginning. It had become common knowledge that the RTC had badly mangled the cleanup of our banks, and in the process, severely damaged our economy.

The only people who could have possibly been surprised by any December announcement after the 1992 elections would have been the voters.

In a scathing 1991 report called "The RTC: Two Years Old and Still Uncertain," the House subcommittee on Financial Institutions

Supervision, Regulation and Insurance released findings from the Resolution Trust Corporation Task Force.

"The Resolution Trust Corporation was designed in crisis," the task force report said. "But the crisis we thought we faced in 1989 has turned out to be almost entirely different from what we face today. In 1989, we thought we would lose $50 billion, but today our losses look more like $200 billion.

"In 1989, it looked like we needed to close 300-400 institutions, but today, we can anticipate closing at least 1,000 financial institutions, and perhaps as many as 1,600."

In its most serious charge, the task force suggested resolution of failed banks had been a kind of hoax.

"In 1989 we thought that resolutions of institutions was our most important activity, but today we know that resolutions are only the veneer. The core is the mountain of eroding assets that linger today in the RTC portfolio having been merely moved from one unsteady environment in failed institutions into an untested, shaky RTC asset disposition program," the House report said.

"In 1989, the RTC was labeled a 'mixed ownership' government corporation, while today we realize that an effort of this size needs some traditional anchors of standard government organization.

"In 1989, we thought the life of the RTC would be short; today we see it will extend beyond the RTC's sunset."

"In 1989, what looked like a capable exclusive manager, the FDIC, has today reported to have such unreliable asset information that its own task of disposing of failed assets is jeopardized."

The bailout had failed.

What it had accomplished was the massive transference of private property from citizens into the hands of an undetermined group of wealthy investors. Our government enabled them to swoop up billions of dollars in assets in the largest corporate takeover in the history of the United States in just a few years. The establishment of the RTC had allowed private entities "to make the profit, leaving any and all risks with the taxpayer," the report said. It was nothing more than an upturned barrel topped with gold sovereigns. The Nothing had chewed a huge hole in the economy; the rescue was just an illusion for another form of greed.

The people who put these plans into place succeeded in consolidating banks into mega-banks, but they never saw the real people they hurt or felt the pain they inflicted.

When was the last time our president, cabinet members or senators traveled coach on a plane, or waited for a seat in a restaurant? Former Defense Secretary Robert McNamara ran the Vietnam War from the Pentagon. When he finished that job, he was moved over to the World Bank. He never had to see, touch, or feel the damage wrought by Vietnam on the rest of us.

The botched bank bailout was no different.

Congressman Bruce Vento of Minnesota, chairman of the RTC Task Force, suggested the bailout was nothing more than a sophisticated scheme; one that is old as Hell.

He said the directors of the RTC were Bush-friendly partisans who used their position as a tool to boost the President's image until the 1992 election. The President's bid for a second term had always faced serious criticism for his lack of leadership during economic crisis.

"I don't think there is any great eagerness on the part of these regulators to begin to close up banks and S&L's across the country. The message . . . would be at odds with the presentation that the economy was on the rebound," he said.

Vento called the RTC a political club-like organization. ". . . As we begin to look at it (RTC), we begin to see it is . . . rife with favoritism and pals. They are not supposed to deal with those who caused the S&L crisis, they are not supposed to benefit from it. And yet we find that the people that they are doing business with, and the people they are selling the property back to are the very people that were responsible for leading the institutions and defaulting on the payments of the loans," said Vento. ". . . They also have to be detached from political interests from the White House. They have demonstrated very often that they are not."

"Instead of taking charge of the issue—here is a major domestic issue—a major impact on the economy—the President is not really taking care of it," Vento said.

Congressman Joseph Kennedy also cited the Executive Office, saying that Congresses' repeated attempts to handle specific problems with the RTC have been too slow.

"These are really management decisions which the Executive Branch of the government is largely responsible for," he said. ". . . it's just an unworkable system. The only way that this can be done is by someone taking an active role in the management."

Both Vento and Kennedy said that the properties being sold are going to wealthy buyers, instead of opening opportunities for the middle class and the poor to buy them. "They are putting together a conglomeration, a big package, and that excludes competition because who can bid on these bulk packages except the biggest financial entities?" Vento says.

"If a lot of poor people get denied access to ownership—hey, that's just part of the problem with the crisis. So rather than getting in and manage a next to impossible job and do the best job we can, we've essentially thrown in the towel," Kennedy said.

"In the end, the bailout was Nothing." said Vento, "Nothing more than an elaborate scheme promoting "the privatization of profit; the socialization of risk."

But that is another story, to be told at another time.

EVIDENCE

EVIDENCE 1

REVIEW AND COMMENT

THE RTC:
TWO YEARS OLD AND STILL UNCERTAIN

Subcommittee on:
Financial Institutions Supervision,
Regulation and Insurance Resolution Trust Corporation
Task Force for the Committee on
Banking, Finance and Urban Affairs
House of Representatives

ONE HUNDERD SECOND CONGRESS
FIRST SESSION
NOVEMBER 23, 1993

Printed for the use of
The Committee on Banking, Finance and Urban Affairs
Submitted by the Chairman of the RTC Oversight Task Force
To the Chairman of the Subcommittee on Financial Institutions
Supervision, Regulation & Insurance

This report has not been officially adopted by the Committee on Banking, Finance and Urban Affairs and may not therefore necessarily reflect the views of its members

U.S. GOVERNMENT PRINTING OFFICE
WASHINGTON : 1991
49-895
For sale by the U.S. Government Printing Office
Superintendent of Documents, Congressional Sales Office
Washington, D.C. 20402
ISBN 0-16-037073-6

LETTER OF TRANSMITTAL
CONGRESS OF THE UNITED STATES
HOUSE OF REPRESENTATIVES
WASHINGTON, DC 20515

October 21, 1991

Honorable Frank Annunzio, Chairman
Subcommittee on Financial Institutions
House Committee on Banking, Finance & Urban Affairs
212 O'Neill House Office Building
Washington, D.C. 20515

Dear Mr. Chairman:

Enclosed please find a copy of the final Chairman's Report of the Financial Institutions subcommittee Task Force on the Resolution Trust Corporation.

I very much appreciate the confidence that you placed in me as Chairman of the Task Force. I believe that the Task Force has played a positive role in holding the Administration and the RTC accountable. While the number of thrifts that have failed is far larger than anyone initially estimated, it is clear that the growing taxpayer costs for the S&L bail-out are due, to a significant degree, to bureaucratic mismanagement and infighting. It is imperative that the Congress, and in particular the Subcommittee on Financial Institutions, keep the public spotlight focused on the RTC.

I look forward to working with you and the other Members of the Subcommittee to accomplish that goal.

Sincerely,
Bruce Vento
Chair, RTC Task Force

cc: Honorable Henry Gonzalez, Chairman, House Committee on

Banking Finance & Urban Affairs

TABLE OF CONTENTS

I. INTRODUCTION

The Resolution Trust Corporation (RTC) was designed in a crisis. But the crisis we thought we faced in 1989 has turned out to be almost entirely different from what we face today. In 1989 we thought we would lose $50 billion, but today our losses look more like $200 billion. In 1989, it looked like we needed to close 300-400 institutions, but today we can anticipate closing at 1,000 financial institutions, and perhaps as many as 1,600. In 1989 we thought that resolutions of institutions was our most important activity, but today we know that resolutions are only the veneer. The core is the mountain of eroding assets that linger today in the

RTC portfolio having been merely moved from one unsteady environment in failed institutions into an untested, shaky RTC asset disposition program. In 1989 the RTC was labeled a "mixed ownership" government corporation, (although there is no private investment in it and, for that matter, no government "investment" is allowed), while today we realize that an effort of this size needs some traditional anchors of standard government organization. In 1989 we thought the life of the RTC would be short; today we see it will extend beyond the RTC's sunset. In 1989, what looked like a capable "exclusive manager" the FDIC, has today been reported to have such unreliable asset information that its own task of disposing of failed bank assets is jeopardized.

These illusions have cost us time and money. They have slowed the schedule of taking institutions into RTC covservatorship, resulted in the failure to collect information to establish values, and tallied sales when all that they may have been achieved was a qualified sale or agreement to accept a "cash flow" mortgage-a joint venture with an option for the private party to put the asset back to the government after private gains through syndication fees, management fees, and tax deductions. The entity makes the "profit", leaving any and all risk with the taxpayer-the privatization of profit; the socialization of risk.

II. SUMMARY OF TASK FORCE ACTIVITY

On May 20, 1991 the Task Force on the RTC (Task Force) held an oversight hearing on asset disposition and the status and effectiveness of the Standard Asset Management and Disposition Program (SAMDA). The matters considered included:

* the number of dollar value of assets in the RTC inventory (including conservatorship and receivership assets);
* the amounts recovered from sales as distinct from amounts collected;

* the proposed use of "cash flow" mortgages;
* the performance of private asset management contractors; and
* the amount of proceeds compared to expected returns.

On June 17, 1991 the Task Force held an oversight hearing to receive testimony from the General Accounting Office concerning the RTC's internal control problems and the implications of these failings for proposals to restructure the bailout effort.
Among the issues considered were:

* the lack of standardized recordkeeping;
* the delays in computerization records and the interrelation of systems; and
* the means for obtaining reasonably accurate asset values.

On July 15, 1991 the Task Force held an oversight hearing to receive expert testimony concerning the structure of the savings and loan bailout.
The specific issues explored included the following:

* whether the standard structure and oversight of Federal agencies in the Executive branch of government would better serve the goals of accountability and least cost than the continuation of the novel structure created under FIRREA;
* whether the usual oversight of Federal agency activities by the Office of Management and Budget would be sufficient, and if not, whether there is some significant purpose for oversight by the Treasury Department;
* which statues and regulations would be applicable to a restructured RTC, as contrasted to the requirements it must now observe; and
* which statutes and regulations would still be of doubtful applicability in a restructured RTC.

The witnesses included the Chairman of the Administrative Conference of the United Sates, persons from the academic community, experts from the GAO, and a representative of the CBO.

On July 26, 1991 the Task Force met again to consider recommendations for the RTC's handling of real estate assets and how the structure of the RTC, among other things, contributed to the inefficiencies of disposing of real estate.

The Task Force has, in addition, obtained counsel from the Institute of Public Administration and the National Academy of Public Administration, organizations respected the world over as possessing extraordinary expertise in matters of government organization, reorganization and structure.

III. THE PROBLEM

Considerable agreement has developed over the past six months that the Resolution Trust Corporation ought to be restructured to facilitate its asset disposition functions. Even the FDIC and the Treasury concede that strong, central direction has been lacking at the RTC.

What led to this widespread realization? Its immediate cause, quite simply, was the combination of vast and steeply increasing costs with agonizingly slow liquidations. More fundamentally, it was the recognition that the task which the RTC is called upon to perform disposal of various assets of institutions that are closed— is significantly different from that originally contemplated by FIRREA. The notion that changes are not appropriate now because the bailout is winding down, should be abandoned.

FIRREA contemplated resolutions of 300-400 institutions with a loss fund cost of $50 billion. By October 1990, the number of failures was assumed to be 600. During the fall, in the face of continuing recession, observers began to predict that additional institutions would fail, perhaps as many as 900. By December 31, 1990, the potential failures were numbered at 1000. Secretary Brady in January 1991, agreed that total resolutions might range between 700 and 1000 institutions.

There are many uncertainties in attempting to estimate the number of institutions that will be closed, but expert opinion is based upon analysis of the types of institutions and the impact of economic conditions on these institutions. The OTS, which has responsibility for regulating privately-held thrifts, that is, those not yet taken over by the government, classifies these institutions in four categories:

* Group I contains well capitalized and profitable thrifts. On June 30, 1991 there were 1,005 such institutions;
* Group II contains institutions that meet or are expected to meet FIRREA's capital requirements, but that are only marginally profitable. On June 30, 1991 there were 716 institutions in this category;
* Group III consists of institutions that are likely to fail, having negative net worth to capital ratios and suffering operating losses each period. On June 30, 1991 there were 377 of these; and
* Group IV consists of institutions that will fail. One June 30, 1991, there were 118 of these.

If all institutions in Group III and Group IV fail, (and many observers expect them to fail) the total additional caseload for the RTC will be 495. Many credible sources, such as the Brookings Institution and the Congressional Budget Office (CBO), have noted that if current adverse economic conditions persist, many institutions classified by the OTS in Group II may also fail. The CBO believes that as many as 70% of the Group II institutions may have to be closed. This would add 501 institutions to the future caseload for a total of 996 institutions over and above the 660 already closed or in the government's hands by June 30, 1991. The additional institutions, by number, constitutes over 45% of what was left of the industry on December 31, 1990.

The resolution caseload, assuming adverse but realistic economic conditions, is half completed. The other component, sales of assets, has only just begun to get underway.

When FIRREA was adopted, Administration estimates assumed that loss in the value of assets would amount to approximately 15% of the total held by failed institutions. After 7 months of operation, the estimated losses on the resolution of 52 RTC-held institutions were $8.5 billion, or 46% of the value of the assets. But Chairman Seidman testified that although losses were higher than predicted, as less distressed institutions were resolved, the figure would be expected to decrease. Through December 31, 1990, the anticipated losses in 352 resolutions averaged 31% of the estimated value of assets, still significantly higher than predicted by Chairman Seidman and the RTC.

Even assuming that RTC Chairman Seidman will eventually be correct that the percentage of loss will be 20% of assets, the net loss on the number of institutions that are expected to fail will be nearly $199 billion, not including the interest carrying costs of all the borrowing needed to finance these losses.

A year ago, GAO stated that the total price (including interest payments) of this effort might range upward from $325 billion. GAO's estimate in the spring of 1991 was $370 billion based on the fact that more institutions will have to be resolved and that less is being returned from asset sales than anticipated. The CBO will not make long-term calculations of Federal borrowing costs because of the nature of Federal debt management, but they did calculate a five year interest cost for $63 billion of additional funding requested by the RTC. At the end of 1996, interest on this amount of RTC borrowing will total $27 billion. It should be noted that these cost estimates only address the post-1989 failures. The pre-1989 failures will cost in excess of $70 billion.

Most of these numbers, however, are estimates based on general expectations rather than actual experience. The RTC has been unable to systematically collect and analyze actual losses on asset sales.

During the past 18 months, the RTC has reduced the prodigious amounts of assets it acquired while closing down institutions, but it is very difficult to know with confidence the magnitude of the accomplishment. Assets sales may take place at three different points in the bailout process during conversatorship, as part of a resolution, or from the receivership. Importantly, the RTC counts collections and repayments of performing loans in its sale totals and while the proper servicing of such loan paper is important it does not reflect the problem assets in the portfolio that represent the bulk of losses. Finally, the data on asset values during conservatorship has not been consistent from month to month.

FDIC Chairman Seidman, in announcing plans to sell $50 billion in assets before the end of the 1990, acknowledge that "...it has taken us a little time to get organized..."

The RTC initially placed its hopes for asset disposition on its contracts with private sector firms using the Standard Asset Management and Disposition Agreement or SAMDA. Like some other RTC efforts, the SAMDA program was significantly delayed. The first contract was not executed until August 30, 1990, one full year after FIRREA was enacted. By May 1991 only preliminary data on asset sales results was available—$0.2 billion sold from the $7.3 billion in real estate held. Eventually proceeds are estimated to be $3.3 billion (45%).

Fully 18 months after the passage of FIRREA, there had been only 2,000 settlements on sales of affordable housing. For purposes of comparison, the Department of Housing and Urban Development in 1989 sold approximately 80,000 single family properties which came into its inventory as a result of mortgage defaults and foreclosures. FNMA typically sells 10,000 properties per year.

The other assets that need to be sold by the RTC, nearly 90% of the total by dollar value, are various securities-mortgages, mortgage pools, junk bonds. These are more liquid and have a more readily determined market value.

In an attempt to speed asset sales, the Oversight Board approved funding for a $7 billion pilot program of seller financing. The sad reality of the seller financing program however is that it merely exchanges one type of asset on the RTC's books for another type of asset. Thus the RTC perpetuates its liabilities, fails to obtain cash to pay down is working capital obligations, and runs risks that the private sector won't take. Secretary Brady testified that even if the RTC must reposes the collateral, the 15% downpayment justifies the effort, but the RTC may make exceptions to the 15% cash requirement. In fact, the actual cash may be as low as 5% because the RTC will allow the cash contributions to be represented by promises to make improvements in the premises and will take a letter of credit for its assurances.

Two other proposed methods for selling assets raise troublesome issues: (1) the cash flow mortgage and (2) the extremely large bulk sale device.

The cash flow mortgage is to be given incident to a sale of property, but as presently structured, it will do little more than get the asset temporarily off the books. The technique envisions sharing in the increased value of a property and profit is measured after a pay back of principal and after deductions for expenses and management fees. There is a significant risk that the RTC will never realize the payment of even the principal-interest payments are already deferred. These cash flow instruments extend for seven years beyond the current lifespan of the RTC. There is a strong likelihood that the asset will come back to the government.

The "grab bag" bulk sale raises another issue-the packages that are being offered are so large that even what the ordinary citizen would consider a large firm cannot bid. These have been recent press reports about a huge sale to G.E. Capital Corp. There is no competition for packages of this size. There may be other disadvantages.

These new initiatives have the unfortunate consequence of circumventing SAMDA contractors and likely causing further delay in a "buyers' market," where purchasers may take a wait and see attitude for further concessions.

Absent a significant change in economic conditions which would change the relative percentage of loss incurred on asset sales, the only element of the problem which is susceptible to modification is the length of time that the government holds the assets, and given that FIRREA already requires that the RTC maximize the net present value return, the focus of improvement must be on those aspects of corporate operation that cause needless delays in collecting and analyzing information and implementing policies. The structure of the organization is a critical determinant of efficient operations and maximum return.

The problem and its cost vastly exceed anything contemplated when FIRREA was adopted. Therefore, the choices of organization and structure in formulating FIRREA can be revisited effectively toady.

IV. MANAGEMENT OF GOVERNMENT ORGANIZATIONS

The evidence of inefficiency in the RTC's operations is overwhelming. The academic discipline of public administration suggests why the structure set out in FIRREA lead to this result. FIRREA created a structure consisting of an Oversight Board, a Resolution Trust Corporation exclusively managed by the Federal Deposit Insurance Corporation, and a Resolution Funding Corporation to serve as a conduit of Federal funds. Fundamental principles of organization recommend a corporate form for those activities of government that involve commercial type activities, but neither the Oversight Board nor the RTC itself were invested with meaningful flexibility that ordinarily follows from corporate organization, nor given the size of the public's obligations, did they become obligated to meaningful accountability.

Board Structure

The RTC must answer to two Boards-the Oversight Board and the Board of FDIC which acting as the RTC's exclusive manager, conducts its day to day operations. The dual board structure had a dubious foundation to begin with.
Chairman Seidman testified in the fall of 1989, saying:

> ....the structure here is a new one, different I think than anything every tried before, exactly this way in government. It involves two separate boards of directors, two separate executive officers, at least two staffs plus the staffs of the various members of the boards. And that means there are a lot more people involved in making decisions and in getting final action than there would be if it were the normal situa- tion where the Congress appropriated to a particular agency. That means, in my view, it is and always will be somewhat slower type of structure. Now, that was put in place because the Administration felt—and I do not question it—that they wanted additional control. And the more controls, and the more people you get involved, then the slower the procedures will be.

Both Boards consist of persons devoting only part-time attention to the operation of the RTC. The Oversight Board is composed of three cabinet-rank officials who have other significant Federal jobs that are equally as demanding of their attention as is the supervision of the RTC. The FDIC Board must regulate and supervise insured banks, many of which are coming to be as troubled financially as the savings and loans which are the responsibility of the RTC.

The National Academy of Public Administration (NAPA) summarized the inadequacies of the situation as follows:

> The present structure violates what are generally considered to be fundamental principles of sound organization. Instead of establishing clear lines of authority and accountability, the authority and accountability for the policies and operations of RTC are divided between the RTC Oversight Board and the Board of Directors of the Federal Deposit Insurance Corporation. The Oversight Board by law is to be held accountable for the RTC, although exclusive authority for management of the corporation is vested in the FDIC. The FDIC board of directors is subject to Oversight Board supervision for some of its functions but not for others. The division of functions among the Oversight Board, FDIC, and RTC inevitably causes confusion, generates conflicts, encourages second-guessing and buck-passing, and make it impossible to hold any one individual or organization accountable for the effective performance of its task assigned to the RTC.

Both the Institute for Public Administration (IPA) and NAPA, advise that a board of directors structure is more suited to deliberative activities rather than commercial type activities; is slower; and diffuses accountability and responsibility. Instead, a single policy making board with a chief executive officer who has direct authority over an operating officer, is more likely a result in efficient organization of an effort such as the bailout. The chief executive officer, appointed by the President and confirmed by the Senate, provides basic leadership and liaison with other parties, while the operating officer reports to the CEO and to the board. The duties of the operating officer are set by the CEO and the board. Placing expertise and operating responsibility in one person eliminates the need for board members to develop large staffs in order to oversee day to day activities. This advice from IPA and NAPA must be taken very seriously.

In addition, the provision of oversight by the Oversight Board rather that the OMB, for example, had added further complications. To take the advice of the Oversight Board is to take the advice of the Department of the Treasurey and that builds in a conflict of interest because the Treasury is not interested in yielding power. The Oversight Board is run by the Treasury. In more than 20 hearings of the Task Force, it has become perfectly clear that top officials of the Treasury Department, below the Secretary, are massively involved in The RTC's operations. Ironically, given the magnitude of the issue and the demand that IPA Review and Comment the Treasury remain involved, the fact is that the Secretary regularly delegates his responsibility for chairing the oversight Board to his subordinates at Treasury.

Management Responsibility

Although FDIC's management may have been thought necessary at the beginning of the bailout, today this management merely adds confusion, uncertainties and costs.

The FDIC has traditional ways of doing business, most of which are inappropriate for the RTC's tasks at hand. Certainly the magnitude of the thrift crisis has grown by at least twice what was anticipated when the present policy was hammered out. The RTC is not in the business of saving institutions. The RTC is not dealing with a few institutions, but is attempting to sell assets-mortgages, loans, securities, real estate.

As indicated by both the IPA and NAPA, the continued management of the RTC by the FDIC is inconsistent with sound management. The FDIC has expertise in running an insurance program and regulating the activities of the insured institutions. It was never designed or intended to supervise a major effort at liquidation. Furthermore, the RTC is disadvantaged by having to rely upon an organization for basic administrative and management services which it cannot control. The RTC is large enough to justify its own system and controls.

In testimony last June before the Senate Banking Committee, Chairman Seidman reiterated his view that the FDIC should no longer be involved in the day to day management of the RTC. He indicated that, "The time has passed when operational control over the RTC by the FDIC board is necessary." He is right because during 1991-92, the FDIC will have to direct its attention to perhaps as many as 400 bank failures, with the Bank Insurance Fund (BIF) that it has sole responsibility to manage.

Corporate Status

The Oversight Board is designated in FIRREA as a "body corporate", as well as an instrumentality of the United States. The RTC is defined in Section 501(b)(2) as follows:

> Notwithstanding the fact that no Government funds may be invested in the Corporation, the Corporation shall be treated, for purposes of sections 9105, 9107, and 9108 of title 3, United States Code, as a *mixed ownership Government corporation which has capital of the Government.* (emphasis added)

As indicated above, the corporate form is traditionally used by the government to provide flexibility in conducting commercial type activities. However, as the IPA and NAPA point out neither entity has a meaningful status as presently structured. The Oversight Board, in fact, conducts no commercial activities-its operations are indistinguishable from those of any other government agency. Furthermore, by calling it an instrumentality, it is allowed to avoid all the protections heretofore though necessary to the prudent operation of a government function.

The RTC does have significant commercial-type activities to conduct, but the effect of FIRREA's provisions for its structure and operation is almost perverse in denying its flexibility that is given to any other government corporation while avoiding the safeguards in management and auditing that necessarily apply to any other government corporation. FIRREA chose the worst of both the government form and the business form.

As indicated in the NAPA letter of August 15, 1991, classifying the RTC as a mixed ownership corporation has significant consequences—it is not subject to certain personnel, procurement, budget and accountability laws (the next section of this commentary details the status that would be applicable to a restructured RTC.) But this designation failed to provide any flexibility of action to the RTC since other legitimate public concerns, led to limits on their actions. On the other hand, the RTC has not given one of the single most important powers of a corporate organization—the ability to determine its expense and how and when they will be satisfied. FIRREA places this responsibility with the Oversight Board. These choices, while giving the appearance of responding to concerns for getting the job done at the least cost, have in fact contributed to the RTC's inability to act efficiently and effectively. Given the substantial public burden for resolving the failure of this industry, the clearer course would have been to designate the RTC a wholly owned government corporation, which is therefore an agency in the executive branch, exempt from statutes only as required by the circumstances of the bailout, with direct authority to do the job.

V. APPLICABLE STATUTES

Redesignating the RTC as an "agency in the executive branch" will not be unduly burdensome or bureaucratic. The RTC is already required to comply with many essential accountability and control laws applicable generally to government entities, and it is the areas where the RTC has been exempted from controls that problems have appeared.

Determining just what kind of agency the RTC is, in its present form, is not readily apparent. The RTC is defined in Section 401(b)(1) of FIRREA as "a Corporation which shall be an instrumentality of the United States." In 501(b)(2) it is further described, as previous indicated, as follows:

> Not withstanding the fact that no Government funds may be invested in the Corporation, the Corporation shall be treated, for purposes of sections 9105, 9107, and 9108 of title 31, United States Code, as a *mixed-ownership Government corporation which has capital of the Government.* (emphasis added)

And if that weren't complicated enough, Section 501(b)(1)(B) of FIREA provides that:

> The Corporation shall be deemed to be an agency of the United Sates for purposes of subchapter II of chapter 5 and chapter 7 of title 51[1], United States Code, when it is acting as a corporation. The Corporation, when it is acting as a conservator or receiver of an insured depository institution, shall be deemed to be any agency of the United States to the same extent as the Federal Deposit Insurance Corporation when it is acting as a conservator or receiver of an insured depository institution.

These are approximately 35 statutes that cover the RTC as "corporation" according to its present description in FIRREA.[2] There are an additional 37 that would be applicable to the RTC as a corporation and as an agency in the executive branch.[3]

The RTC acknowledges that only four types of statutes are significant to the RTC's operations: financial controls; employees; administrative (including procurement); and environmental.

Financial Controls

When the GAO reported earlier this summer that they would not be able to finish their audit of the RTC on time, and that when the audit was issued it would likely be qualified, the RTC began to comply voluntarily with a financial accounting statute that ordinarily is applicable to only designated "executive agencies". This statute, 31 USC ss 3512(b) (formerly known as the Federal Managers' Financial Integrity Act) requires the head of each executive agency to establish and maintain systems of accounting and internal controls that, among other things, provide adequate financial information for management purposes. GAO had reported that the RTC was unable to reconcile the information on assets received from its conservatorship operations and that carried on its centralized information systems.

The Vento proposal for restructuring would end reliance on voluntary action by making the RTC a corporation subject to the rules of accountability under the Government Corporation Control Act for wholly owned government corporations. The consequence is that the RTC's budget is submitted for Congressional review, as are the budgets of other government corporations and it is reviewed first by the Office of Management and Budget. Since the restructuring proposals will eliminate review by the Oversight Board, and thus the Treasury Department, there will be no duplication of effort. Furthermore, it will not impair the funding mechanism set up in FIREA since the statute reserves the rights to carry out or finance"...its activities as authorized under another law."[4] Clearly, the public interest would best be served by compliance with the general array of laws applicable to agencies, rather than finding out 20-months into the effort that an audit cannot be readily obtained.

Employees

The status of RTC's employees derives from the status of the FDIC[5] and the application of the civil service laws, without more, might have consequences in two area; rates of pay would be lower at each grade level, and temporary status of employees could be eliminated. The Federal Deposit Insurance Act was adopted prior to civil service reform and that subsequent reform legislation did not amend the FDIC. Consequently, although the FDIC is subject to the civil service laws it retains independent authority to set the wage levels for its' employees. Particularly in recent years, the levels have been higher than the schedule applicable to general civil servants. The restructuring legislation continues the authority for the RTC to set rates of pay.[6] The authority to hire temporary employees results from a waiver which the FDIC obtained from the Office of Personnel Management. There is no prohibition in the Vento restructuring legislation that would prevent the RTC from obtaining a similar waiver.

Procurement

Over the past 2 years, the RTC has struggled to develop procurement regulations and policies that are tailored to the task it must perform. Designating the RTC as an agency in the executive branch will bring the RTC under the requirement applicable to all other civilian and military agencies. There are two matters to note. Section 744(f) of FIRREA grants an exception to the RTC from the requirements of the Federal Property and Administrative Services Act for the disposal of "...residential property, or of other property (real or personal) held as part of or acquired for or in connection with residential property, or in connection with the insurance of mortgages, loans, or savings association accounts under the ...Federal Deposit Insurance Act or any other law." Since this is not changed by designating the RTC as an agency in the executive branch, only the RTC's purchases of goods and services would be affected by the restructuring.

The impact of bringing the RTC under the procurement laws[7] cannot be reasonably judged by considering purchases in the aggregate, but can only be illuminated by considering different types of purchases by the RTC. It is not useful to allege merely that the procurement laws will add delays in general and, therefore, are unacceptable in the context of any effort that has a definite and rapidly approaching end date. Purchases of computers and of asset management and disposition services provide examples. The RTC has attempted for almost a year to develop and implement a comprehensive information management system, which as it appears more and more clearly, was a key factor needed to make the RTC successful. Those systems are not yet fully operational. Had the RTC been an agency subject to the Brooks Act, we might have had better control of the process. In any event, the major equipment buys have been made, so that the supplementation of the overall system can certainly not be said to be impaired by honoring the Brooks Act at this time.

The methods adopted for the acquisition of services, such as Standard Asset Management and Disposition contracts, were not developed so rapidly[8] that an argument can be credible that suggests that the authorization in FIRREA is faster than any procedure under the standard procurement statutes. The standard procurement laws, furthermore, have other benefits. Some which come to mind are the fair sharing of contracts with women and minorities and the protection of small business.

The recent disclosure of inappropriate, sensational costs associated with trinkets, artworks and furniture, and the "Martinelli" affair, cost the RTC more in credibility than any inconvenience attendant to following reasonable safeguards inherent in the procurement laws applicable throughout the national government and its' agencies.

The Chairman of the Government Operations Committee has advised that they are very concerned that the RTC has not been subject to the procurement laws. Chairman Conyers writes.

There is nothing unique about the mission or operations of RTC that would justify continued exemption. Certainly RTC's status as a "financial" agency does not provide justification for exempting it from controls, for example, how it buys its' typewriters or pencils. With respect to procurement, RTC is no different than any other executive agency and should not be treated differently.

Environmental Laws

In regard to environmental concerns the capacity in which the RTC is acting is more important than in regard to employees and procurement. The RTC through its conservatorship and receivership activities will control a vast amount of real estate (although this does not represent the greatest proportion of the value of assets). The RTC has avoided taking title to any properties in its corporate capacity.[9] Its status as a conservator or receiver is a different matter. The RTC relies upon the fact that in neither instances does it take technical title, even though it has the power and authority to sell and convey and to control the receipt and disposition of the proceeds. This argument is more persuasive in the context of conservatorships because there is still a separate, operating entity. As to receiverships, however, the argument that the RTC is like any ordinary court appointed receiver or trustee is not credible. The governments' investment in the savings and loan bailout is massive. By the time the assets are sold and proceeds are available to be distributed, the government will be a creditor holding claims that amount to 90 to 99 percent of the total claims. Given this reality, the balance between environmental gains or making money for other creditors, tips decidedly in favor of environmental responsibility. It also follows that for those dispositions which take place from the conservatorship which are pursuant to future receivership powers, that is, when an asset is packaged for sale with assets from other institutions for bulk sale, then the environmental laws should apply.

The impact of environmental responsibility varies with each act.

The National Environmental Policy Act (NEPA) requires agencies of the Federal government to evaluate the environmental consequences of major federal actions, and by implication, moderate these consequences to the extent practicable. Not all sales of land by the RTC in any of its capacities would be a "major" Federal action. The RTC might, in doubtful situations, have to conduct environmental assessments, but these are neither as extensive or time consuming as an impact statement.

The Endangered Species Act also applies to federal actions, but contemplates only consultation with the Fish and Wildlife Service which might result in deed restrictions on land use.

The Comprehensive Environmental Response, Compensation and Liability Act (CERCLA) requires the identification of potential hazardous contamination of properties, and depending on the circumstances, the assessment and cleanup of such conditions.

The Lead-Base Paint Act (LPPPA) contains similar notice, assessment and cleanup obligations as CERCLA.

There are two executive orders which would become applicable to the RTC as an agency in the executive branch -E.O. 11988 on flood plain management and E.O. 11990 on wetlands protection. In general, these orders require that consideration be given to the effects of construction on, or disposition of wetlands and flood plains. Deed restrictions may be the outcome.

The National Historic Preservation Act requires the identification of historically significant properties and consultation with historic preservation groups.

Such information and compliance can actually be helpful to facilitate the disposition of assets, avoiding possible litigation and avoiding abortive sales efforts. Too often RTC sales attempts have demonstrated a lack of understanding of basic environmental limits on specific assets.

VI. ALTERNATIVES TO RESTRUCTURING

The Treasury believes that no statutory restructuring is needed. Its' notion is that simply hiring a strong CEO will solve the purely "operational" difficulties that have plagued the RTC since its initial organization in August 1989. Candidly, that concept already failed when the Oversight Board's first President, Dan Kearney, left in frustration in early 1990. The Chairman of the FDIC, Bill Seidman believes that restructuring is needed. In his appearance before the Subcommittee on Financial Institutions Supervision, Regulations and Insurance on September 12, 199, he proposed changes that he said had the concurrence of the Secretary of the Treasury. With all respect to Chairman Seidman, the result looks more like the conclusion of a turf battle in which the solution was to allow both sides to get more of what they wanted. Reading between the lines, straightening up the RTC to get it working most efficiently and effectively is not the point of that proposal.

While relieving the Oversight Board of some responsibilities, the proposed legislation creates a huge loophole for the Oversight

Board to demand the modification of the RTC's rules and other pronouncements that it deems "...materially inconsistent with overall strategies...the policies or purposes of applicable law, or with the efficient and economical discharge of the Corporation's duties, or with sound public policy." Furthermore, the Oversight Board is not abolished, but is enlarged with non-voting members. The legislation also fails to clear up the anomaly of a board which is called a mixed ownership government corporation, but has no private investment, conducts no commercial-type activities, and the majority of whom are full time government employees.

Similarly, while ostensibly removing the FDIC as the exclusive manager, the legislation leaves the FDIC board intact as the Board of the RTC, except for adding two members, the CEO of the RTC and a representative of the Oversight Board. It is difficult to see how this structure will contribute to clear lines of authority and accountability and greater efficiency. The legislation then goes on to provide that the CEO will be an employee of the FDIC on loan to the RTC who will be selected by the Oversight Board.

The solution to the RTC's problems requires more.

VII. CONCLUSIONS AND RECOMMENDATIONS

In the last report on the activities of the RTC, I recommended changes in its structure and internal operations. I, and other members of this committee, have introduced legislation to address the structural flaws. The minimum elements of the revision I have suggested include (1) replacing the dual boards with a single board; (2) removing the FDIC as exclusive manager; (3) setting up a position for a CEO with the responsibility and background to get the job done, who will be appointed by the President and confirmed by the Senate; and (4) clarifying the status of the RTC as an agency in the executive branch of the government. There is only one additional point to be made about structural changes. The experts have told us that there is nothing about this bailout that requires the close involvement and control by the Treasury Department. This kind of control is ordinarily exercised by the OMB, for every other type of government agency.

The GAO has provided testimony indicating that an oversight board is important given the size of the government's financial commitment. In conversations with the staff at the GAO we determined that their concern is that some sort of oversight body is designated, but not that it needs to have the powers of the present oversight board. They do not feel that the Treasury Department must be involved. However, if there are two boards and no involvement of the Treasury, it follows that both be appointed by the President. This in turn, in my opinion, could lead to unnecessary friction between two entities that each believe they have an independent route to the President. A better arrangement would be to have the President appoint the CEO, and then the board and the CEO would appoint the chief operating officer.

There is an issue related to structure, but not strictly the structure of the RTC. If the RTC is restructured as I suggest, then consideration should be given to transferring the liquidation functions that the FDIC performs for banks to the RTC.

Improving Operations

Although this report has been concerned primarily with structural issues, there are some operational changes that the RTC itself should make as soon as possible. If the RTC cannot or will not accomplish these changes, we must seriously consider giving them a statutory directive.

While the RTC has made some progress with its' management information systems, the task is far from complete. There is a need for extraordinary care in entering the data into the RTC's management information systems. In order to assure this, the RTC needs a central computer that is available for use by all levels of the organization. There must be prompt input of new data, and updates of information at all data collection points along with proper safeguards and verification. The points of collection that the RTC must pay attention to include the law firms that handle litigation or collection work for the RTC; the SAMDA contractors who are tasked with management and sale of selected assets; the administrative and financial operations within conservatorships and receiverships; and the RTC's financial offices. I have attached as Exhibit B, a copy of my letter to Chairman Seidman outlining my concerns about data collection.

Furthermore, there are still serious questions about whether the system which the RTC is developing will be sufficiently interconnected so that information can be sorted and retrieved in all the situations where it is needed. For example, the system ought to allow any office of the RTC to track assets and match their characteristics with bids on contracts, so that if a bidder had a prior interest in the asset the appropriate action can be taken.

With regard to asset sales, there are two immediate steps that the RTC can take. First, all the assets located in a metropolitan area should be sold by local offices of the RTC, no matter what institution initially held title or interest in them. The only exception to this policy would be those assets, such as hotel or shopping centers, that are typically marketed nationwide. Second, the RTC ought to consider mandatory auctions. The only basis for not concluding a sale would be the lack of sufficient bidders to assume a competition. The hesitancy of a temporary bureaucracy to make sales in order to preserve their role is not solved by turning the decision over to private contractors, since the same sort of incentive operates to keep the contract alive.

With regard to saving money, the RTC should end the policy of rolling over brokered deposits in conservatorships. This is an example of how the dual board structure has led to waste and inefficiency. The RTC has been asking the Oversight Board for funds to pay these deposits off, but the Oversight Board has no definitive policy and hasn't given the necessary authority to borrow from the Federal Financing Bank to replace these high cost funds with low cost funds. One snapshot, taken on July 31, 1991 illustrates the problem paying 50 to 100 basis points extra, generates fees paid on brokered deposits of $37 million on $7.8 billion of deposits. It doesn't help to realize that the refusal has its' political benefits that is, as long as the brokered deposits are rolled over the cost is not reflected as a cost of the U.S. taxpayers. But the bottom line is apparent, the final cost to the taxpayers is compounded when it does appear on the books.

With regard to saving, the RTC should structure more of its' resolutions as insured deposit transfers. There is very little franchise value that can be realized, so little in fact, that the benefits are wasted by the delays in arranging other types of resolutions.

With regard to saving money, and avoiding continued government involvement, the RTC should limit its use of cash flow mortgages.

With regard to saving money, the RTC needs to be authorized to contract with or delegate to other government agencies any one of its assets disposition tasks. For example, the RTC which has closed less than 4,000 sales on single family affordable houses, could transfer its' rights in these properties to HUD, which has some significant sales successes with similar properties. Other agencies are equipped to help in the RTC with these specialized activities.

With regard to saving money, the RTC needs to evaluate and cap the amounts that it pays for outside legal services. It is certainly unprecedented, and unwarranted for the government to pay $600 per hour for legal services an amount considerably in excess of fees paid in the private sector.

With regard to assuring the taxpayers that their funds are being wisely spent, the RTC must become more vigilant in hiring employees of failed savings and loan institutions, to assure that those who contributed to the problem, do not benefit from its solution.

Finally, a detailed analysis of the real estate assets and real estate markets for each type of asset locations, demographics, economies of operation is needed. Given sufficient information, the RTC would be able to decide whether the land should be sold or held. For lands that should be held in the inventory, management could be patterned after the Bureau of Land Management. The RTC needs to couple analysis with timely, reliable information. Otherwise, we cannot even begin to estimate our costs for this unwelcome and unprecedented public undertaking.

Congressional Oversight

The record of the past two years makes one fact abundantly clear. Congress needs to exercise continuous, conscientious oversight of the RTC. FIRREA created an Oversight Board that was to assure efficiency and effectiveness, among other things. Its' records of oversight is not reassuring. Congress asked that the RTC take environmental concerns into account in disposing of repossessed properties, but the RTC's efforts to work with the government agency with expertise in these matters was thwarted. Congress asked that minority and women contractors be given consideration for a fair proportion of the private sector contracting of the RTC. The "interim final" regulations for this program were just published. Congress directed that a Strategic Plan be developed to assure that serious attention was devoted to those operating activities that would bring about a speedy conclusion to the task. But the management information system that should have been a key part of the Strategic Plan has yet to become fully operational. Most recently we learned that the RTC had stayed in competition with private sector thrifts, healthy private sector thrifts by paying premium interest to retain brokered deposits. We had thought that they disavowed this practice of using high cost brokered deposits to keep the doors open. Apparently that wasn't the case and we have lost uncounted sums of the public's money and created unfair competition for the industry.

Clearly the quality of oversight we expected has not been provided. This means that Congress has to take a special responsibility for seeing that the effort is going well. For the past two years, the Task Force on the RTC has been the only formal oversight for this multi-billion dollar program in either body. The Task Force on the RTC has had little in committee resources to review all of the critical issues although it has had the full cooperation of both the General Accounting Office and the Congressional Budge Office, and the membership of the Banking Committee.

VIII. FOOTNOTES FOR THE REVIEW AND COMMENT

1. These chapters cover administrative procedures and judicial review.

2. Government corporation Control Act (31 USC 9101-9110); 42 USC ss 2000e (Equal Employment Opportunity); Inspector General Act (5 USC ss ss1 12, Appendix 3); Administrative Procedures Act (5 USC ss ss701-706); Clean Wate Act (33 USC ss ss 1251-1376); Coastal Barrier Resources Act (16 USC ss 3504, et. seq.); Coastal Barrier Improvement Act of 1990 (12 USC ss ss1441a-3); Comprehensive Environmental Response, Compensation & Liability Act (42 USC ss 9601); Endangered Species Act

(16 USC ss ss 1531-1544); Equal Access to Justice Act (28 USC ss 2412); Federal Tort Claims Act (28 USC ss 2671, et. seq.); Freedom of Information Act (5 USC ss 552); Lead Based Paint (42 USC ss ss 4821-4846); Migratory Bird Conservation Act (16 USC ss ss 701-711); National Historic Preservation Act (16 USC ss 470, et. seq.); Privacy Act (5 USC ss 552a); Regulatory Flexibility Act (5 USC ss ss 601-612); Resource Conservation and Recovery Act (42 USC ss ss 6901-697); Safe Drinking Water Act (42 USC ss ss 300f-300j-26); Toxic Substances Control Act (15 USC ss 2601, et. seq.); Government in the Sunshine (5 USC ss 552b); Drug Free Workplace Act (41 USC ss ss701707); Fair Credit Reporting Act (15 USC ss ss 1681-16811); 31 USC ss 1352 (Use of appropriate funds to influence contracts); Spending Reduction Act of 1984 (26 USC ss 6402); Spending Reduction Act (31 USC ss 3702A); 31 USC ss 1344 (Use of Government vehicles); Federal Financing Bank Act (12 USC ss ss 2281-2296); Securities Exchange Act of 1934 (15 USC ss ss 78a-78kk); 18 USC ss 6 (Various ethics, conflict of interest, fraud prohibitions); 28 USC ss 451 (Various government litigation requirements); Government Employee Training Act (5 USC ss ss 4101-4118); Public Buildings Act (40 USC ss ss 601-619); Public Buildings Cooperative Use Act (40 USC ss 490); Energy Conservation *n Production Act (42 USC ss ss 6831-6840).

3. If defined as a wholly owned government corporation and an agency in the executive branch, the following additional laws would apply to the RTC: Brooks Act (40 USC ss 759); Civil Service Reform Act (5 USC ss ss 2302, 3327(b)); Senior Executive Service (5 USC ss ss 3131-3596); Performance Rating Act (5 USC ss ss 4301-4308); Competitions in Contracting Act (41 USC ss ss 252, et seq.); Contract Disputes Act (41 USC ss ss601-613); Federal Property and Administrative Services Act (40 USC ss

471, et. seq.); Federal Records Act (44 USC ss 3301, et. seq.); National environmental Policy Act (42 USC ss ss 4321-4347); Office of Federal Procurement Policy Act (41 USC ss ss 401-420); Paperwork Reduction Act (44 USC ss 3510); Tucker Act (non-financial claims against the US) (28 USC ss 1491); 31 USC ss 717 (program evaluation); 31 USC ss 720 (Agency reports); Prompt Payment Act (31 USC ss ss 3901-3907); Program Information Act (31 USC ss ss 61016105); Age Discrimination Act (42 USC ss ss 6101-6107); National Energy Conservation Policy Act (42 USC ss ss 8251-8259); Stewart B. McKinney Homeless Act (42 USC ss ss 11311-11320); Power plant and Industrial Fuel Use Act (42 UC ss ss 8301, 8484); Hatch Act (5 USC ss ss 1501-1508); Thrift Institution Restructuring Act (12 USC ss 1701j-3, et. seq.); Truth-in-Lending (15 USC ss ss 16011667e); Securities Act of 1933 (15 USC ss ss 77a-77aa); 31 USC ss 3701-3733 (Claims against US); Contract Work Hours (40 USC ss ss 329-333); Anti-Kickback Enforcement Security Act (15 USC ss ss 51-058); 44 USC ss ss 501, 5 04, 1103, 1106, 1108, 11110 (Use of Government Printing Office); Computer Security Act (15 USC ss 278g-3); Copeland Act (kickbacks) (18 USC ss 874); Davis Bacon Act (40 USC ss ss 276a, 276c); Program Fraud Civil Remedies Act (31 USC ss ss 3801-3812); Debt Collection Act (5 USC ss 5514); Federal Insecticide, Fungicide & Rodenticide Act (7 USC ss 136, et. seq.); Assignment of Claims (41 USC ss 15; 31 USC ss 3727); Service Contract Act (41 USC ss ss 351-358).

4. 31 USC ss 9104(b)(1)

5. Section 501(b)(9)(A) of FIRREA provides that the RTC shall have no employees. During the time that the FDIC is the exclusive managing agent, the RTC makes reimbursement for services rendered by FDIC employees.

6. A strong argument can be made that higher wage levels for RTC

employees are not justified. These recent exceptions for increased wage levels were based on the perceived need to retain experienced examiners in financial regulatory agencies. RTC, however, is not such a regulatory agency; it is a liquidation agency.

7. These laws include the Brooks Act (4USC ss 759); the Competition in Contracting Act (41 USC ss 252, et. seq.); the Contract Disputes Act (41 USC ss ss 601-613); the Office of Federal Procurement Policy Act (41 USC ss ss 401-420); and the Federal Property and Administrative Services Act (40 USC ss 471, et. seq.)

8. The first agreements were not executed until January 1991, about 17 months after the RTC officially began business.

9. It has voluntarily issued notices under some environmental laws while at the same time arguing that the laws do not apply.

EVIDENCE 2

UNITED STATES GENERAL ACCOUNTING OFFICE

BRIEFING REPORT TO:

THE CHAIRMAN,
COMMERCE, CONSUMER, AND MONETARY AFFAIRS SUBCOMMITTEE,
COMMITTEE ON GOVERNMENT OPERATIONS,
HOUSE OF REPRESENTATIVES
Resolution Trust Corporation

Better Qualified Review Appraisers Needed
GAO/GGD-92-40BR
GAO United States General Accounting Office
Washington, D.C. 20548
General Government Division
B-248151
April 23, 1992
The Honorable Doug Barnard, Chairman,
Commerce, Consumer and Monetary Affairs Subcommittee
Committee on Government Operations
House of Representatives

Dear Mr. Chairman:

On January 31, 1992, you asked us to look at several aspects of the appraisal reforms contained in Title XI of the Financial Institutions Reform, Recover, and Enforcement Act of 1989. At that time, we were assessing the qualifications of the Resolution Trust Corporation's (RTC) in-house review appraisers. We briefed the Subcommittee staff on the results of this work on March 27, 1992. This briefing report contains the information we presented.

Since August 1989, RTC has ordered over 100,100 appraisals

for the real estate under its control. Review appraisers are technical specialists employed by RTC to administer the asset valuation process. They fulfill a key internal control function that includes monitoring outside appraisers selection, reviewing appraisals done by contract appraisers, and helping execute RTC's asset appraisal and valuation policies. They also serve as internal consultants on appraisal issues. This highly qualified review appraisers are needed to protect the government's interests in valuating and selling assets.

In these briefing report we asses the qualifications of the review appraisers that RTC hired between October 8, 1989, and June 3, 1991. We did this assessment because (1) we were concerned about asset valuation in general, (2) past appraisal-related problems had contributed to the thrift crisis, and (3) faulty appraisals could have a significant effect on the overall thrift bailout cost.

RESULTS IN BRIEF

RTC's approach to hiring in-house review appraisers gave regional and consolidated field office selecting officials much discretion in identifying the most qualified candidates among applicants. Other than a general job description, RTC had no specific hiring criteria to guide these officials in this process.

Our analysis shows that 69 percent of RTC's review appraisers do not appear to be adequately qualified for their positions because they did not have enough appraisal experience. This condition weakens RTC's assurance that contract appraisals are reasonable and done properly. We believe a root cause for this condition is the lack of adequate hiring standards or criteria for these positions, coupled with RTC's practice of not requiring applicants to submit enough supporting data on their appraisal education and experience.

More specifically, RTC headquarters has not provided leadership to its' field offices in setting review appraiser qualification standards and hiring criteria. Further, management has not been evaluating the performance of these staff in carrying out RTC's appraisal activities. We believe these weaknesses have resulted in RTC hiring underqualified individuals.

To improve its in-house appraisal review capabilities, we are recommending that RTC (1) hire a senior executive level chief appraiser to manage and assess the appraisal program's execution, (3) assess the appraisal skills and capabilities of the current review appraiser staff, (3) upgrade the skills and capabilities of any underqualified review appraisers as rapidly as feasible, (4) develop and implement detailed qualification standards and hiring criteria to ensure that qualified personnel are hired, and (5) require more complete data from applicants to support their appraisal-related educational background and experience. OBJECTIVE, SCOPE, AND METHODOLOGY

Our goal was to determine whether RTC had qualified review appraisers to meet its highly complex real estate valuation needs. To do this, we developed composite assessment criteria, determined the education and experience of RTC's review appraisers, compared these factors to the criteria, and identified those individuals that did not appear to meet the assessment criteria based on their level of education and experience, both general and appraisal-related. We also contacted over 30 private sector appraisers to solicit their views of RTC's appraisal practices.

To help us develop the criteria and evaluate review appraisers' qualifications, we used an appraisal consultant. In developing our composite criteria, we considered the Appraisal Foundation's and Office of Personnel Management's published qualification criteria. We discussed with eight agencies the criteria they use for hiring appraisers. We also discussed our composite criteria with several senior RTC review appraisers, who generally concurred with the criteria. Our consultant's assessments included an overall ranking, as well as detailed rankings for education, general experience, and appraisal experience.

We assessed the qualifications of 51 review appraisers listed in RTC's July 1, 1991, National Directory of Review Appraisal Staff, RTC headquarters. We used their job applications to get data on education level and extent of work experience. We independently assessed the accuracy of some information given in job applications. For example, we contacted the Appraisal Institute to verify statements that the appraiser was a member or had a professional designation.

Besides the data from the job applications, we used other readily available information such as resumes, job interview documentation, and qualification statements. Since the education and experience data required considerable professional knowledge to interpret, our consultant assessed the qualifications of all the individuals. In many cases, applications did not give complete data. In cases where the missing data could possibly have influenced the assessment, other experienced appraisers who were familiar with the individual's past experience were contacted.

We assessed experience at the time the individuals were hired. We did not assess their performance while at RTC.

We contacted officials and reviewed records from RTC headquarters and eight consolidated field offices (Kansas City, Baton Rouge, Somerset, Atlanta, Cost Mesa, Dallas, Chicago, and Philadelphia) between July 1991 and March 1992. During this period we also contacted appraisal officials at all four RTC regional offices (Atlanta, Dallas, Kansas City, and Denver). Our work was done in accordance with generally accepted government auditing standards.

We discussed the contents of this report with appropriate RTC headquarters officials. We have incorporated their views where appropriate. RTC officials told us that the high demand for appraisers at the time RTC was recruiting employees may have affected their ability to hire quality employees. They also expressed concern about our methodology in assessing review appraisers, although they acknowledged that they did have some underqualified review appraisers on the staff.

While we agreed that our methodology would have been stronger had we used a panel of three consultants to do the technical assessment, we believe our assessment methodology was strong enough to demonstrate that RTC has serious weaknesses. We also believe that the results of the assessment would not have changed significantly due to the lack of adequate information on the applicant's prior experience in personnel files.

We also discussed our findings with selected regional and consolidated field office officials. Their views have also been incorporated where appropriate.

We are sending copies of this briefing report to other interested congressional Committees and Members of Congress; Chairman, Thrift Depositor Protection Oversight Board; and Chief Executive Officer and President, RTC. We will also make copies available to others upon request.

This report was prepared under the direction of Ronald L. King, Assistant Director, Federal Management Issues. Other major contributors to this briefing report are listed in appendix III. If you have any questions, please contact me at (202) 736-0479.

Sincerely yours,

Gaston L. Gianni, Jr.
Associate Director
Federal Management Issues

CONTENTS

ABBREVIATIONS

CFO - consolidated field office
CPE - continuing professional education
FIRREA - Financial Institutions Reform, Recovery, and Enforcement Act of 1989
IG - Inspector General
MAI - Member, Appraisal Institute
OPM - Office of Personnel Management
RTC - Resolution Trust Corporation
VA - Veterans Administration

ASSESSMENT OF RTC'S REVIEW
APPRAISERS' QUALIFICATIONS BACKGROUND

* Review Appraiser Activities
* Effects of Faulty Appraisals
* Role of Review Appraisers
* Past Concerns About Appraisers
* Hiring of Review Appraisers
* Recent Personnel Developments

BACKGROUND

Activities of RTC Review Appraisers

The Resolution Trust Corporation (RTC) considers an asset's appraised value when considering its' sale, and hires contract appraisers to prepare appraisals. This appraisal work is complex because RTC's properties are of diverse types, such as land, residential, and commercial, and are located throughout the country. Also, in many cases its' properties are of poor quality and cannot be easily valued and current real estate market conditions are very unsettled and thus, very difficult to assess.

As a very heavy user of appraisal services, RTC is highly vulnerable to abuses in the appraisal process. As of December 31, 1991, RTC's inventory included real estate assets with an estimated book value of $16.7 billion, and delinquent loans of all types valued at $26.4 billion. The real estate that secures some of these delinquent loans must be periodically appraised until the loans are sold or foreclosed. As more thrifts are placed under RTC control, its inventory of real estate and delinquent loans will continue to grow. Since August 1989, RTC has ordered over 100,100 appraisals.

Thus, it is important that RTC be able to ensure that faulty appraisals do not adversely affect the value of its assets and the amount realized when they are sold.

Potential Effects of Faulty Appraisals

Faulty appraisals can have at least two adverse effects on RTC. If appraisals are too high, estimated recovery values and sales prices will be set too high and the property may not sell. This scenario increases both holding costs and the need for loss funds, thereby increasing the cost of the bailout. If appraisals are too low, property may be sold for less than it is worth. This scenario also increases the need for more loss funds.

Role of Review Appraisers

RTC's in-house review appraisers fulfill a key internal control function. Appraisals done by contract appraisers are reviewed by RTC's review appraisers for technical competency as well as compliance with contractual requirement. These appraisers also monitor the appraisal contractor selection process and serve as technical advisors to RTC officials in formulating and interpreting asset valuation and disposal policies. They also advise on the actual disposal of specific properties.[1]

Past Concerns About Appraisers

In 1986, a House Government Operations Committee report concluded that "Faulty and fraudulent real estate appraisals have become an increasingly serious national problem. Their harmful effects are widespread, pervasive, and costly. They have seriously damaged and contributed directly to the insolvency of hundreds of the Nation's financial institutions and have helped cause billions of dollars in losses to lenders, private mortgage insurers, investors, and federal insurance funds. Responsibility for this problem rests with those who perform appraisals or base lending and related mortgage insurance/investment decisions on appraisals they know or should have known were improper or inaccurate."[2]

Work done by both us and various agency Inspectors General

(IG) verify the Committee's conclusion. Over the past 5 years we have issued 14 reports raising concerns about various appraisal practices and abuses. We expressed concern about agency internal controls, quality of appraisals, methodologies used, and the ethics of appraisers who did the work. Our reports are listed in "Related GAO Products."

In 1985, the Department of Housing and Urban Development IG found "significant departures from departmental requirements in the areas of recruitment, selection, work assignment, and monitoring of fee personnel." The study noted that these conditions were "largely the same as those found in a 1978 nationwide audit." Also in 1985, the Veterans Administration (VA) IG reported that original home loan guarantee program appraisals frequently overvalued properties and that almost 10 percent VA's approved appraisers had been suspended or removed during fiscal year 1985. RTC's IG has a series of audits in process on its appraisal contracting practices. Reports on these audits should be issued later this fiscal year.

[1]RTC's review appraisers also oversee decisions on whether to sell delinquent loans or to foreclose and then sell the property.

[2]Committee on Government Operations. Forty-Eighth Report: Impact of Appraisal Problems on Real Estate Lending, Mortgage Insurance, and Investment in the Secondary Market, House Report 99-891, 99th Congress, 2nd Session (Washington, D.C., Sept. 25, 1986).

APPENDIX I

How RTC Hires, Reviews Appraisers and Criteria Used

Most of the current in-house review appraisers came to RTC in late 1989 and 1990 when the agency was growing quite rapidly. Other than a general job description, RTC had no specific hiring criteria. Selecting officials had discretion in identifying the most qualified candidates from among applicants. Information about the most qualified was sent to RTC regional administrative officers to determine whether they met the general qualification criteria of the Federal Deposit Insurance Corporation.

Recent Personnel Developments

During 1991 and 1992, RTC experienced difficulty in retaining its' appraisal staff. Seven senior appraisers, including three that our assessment concluded were qualified, and six review appraisers left during 1991. Of the 13, 5 were either terminated by RTC for ethics reasons or resigned while being investigated.

The loss of review appraisers left two consolidated field offices (CFO) with no appraisers for at least part of 1991. The New Jersey office, which was without an appraiser for about 1 month, has filled one vacant position and will be hiring at least one more appraiser. The Baton Rouge office, which was without a full-time appraiser for 9 months, has also hired a replacement appraiser.

Existing Appraiser Criteria Appraisal Foundation

- 165 hours of classroom training
- 10 CPE hours annually
- 2,000 hours of experience

EXISTING APPRAISER CRITERIA

Appraisal Foundation

The Appraisal Foundation's education and experience qualification criteria has different certification levels; the certified general real property appraisers is the highest skill level. We discuss qualifications here only for this highest designation, since the work these appraisers do most closely resembles RTC's. Foundation guidelines, however, do not address the review function so essential to RTC.

Beginning in January 1992, state-certified appraisers must be used on federal-related transactions. These appraisers must meet the requirements for certifications issued by the Appraisal Foundation. The certifying offices of 18 states have already implemented this requirement.

Education

The Foundation's certified general real estate property appraiser criteria require 165 classroom hours in subjects related to real estate appraisal and continuing professional education (CPE) training equivalent to 10 hours per year. The criteria also require that qualifying education include such topics as economic principles, valuation process, sales comparison approach, and narrative report writing. Credit toward the CPE requirement is awarded for teaching appraisal courses.

Experience

The Foundation requires at least 2,000 hours of work experience spread over a minimum 2-year period. Also, at least 50 percent of the qualifying experience must be in nonresidential appraisal work to ensure a variety of experience. Hours of experience are required rather than years to prevent occasional or relatively simple appraisal experience from being used to qualify. Acceptable experience includes, but is not limited to, fee and staff appraisals, ad valorem tax appraisals, review appraisals, appraisal analysis, real estate counseling, highest and best use analysis, feasibility analysis/study, and teaching appraisal courses.

Existing Appraiser Criteria, OPM, and Eight Agencies

* OPM standards
* College degree/work experience
* Progressive work experience
* Agency requirements
* Varied considerably
* RTC does not have criteria

Office of Personnel Management

The Office of Personnel Management (OPM) gives federal agencies generic appraiser qualification standards; agencies set their own hiring standards. OPM calls for a college degree at the grade 5 or 7 entry level or 3 years of experience, and progressively more education and/or experience for higher grade levels. For example, a grade 14 appraiser should have at least 5 years of increasingly more advanced or complex appraisal experience.

Federal Agencies

Agency hiring criteria differ among the eight agencies we contacted. The Department of Justice and General Services Administration, for example, use only the (OPM qualification standards. The Army Corps of Engineers requires at least 2 appraisal courses and 5 years of experience, while the Forest Service, for example, requires 60 hours over a 3-year period, while the Department of Transportation does not have a CPE requirement. Four agencies do not have written standards describing their education and experience criteria; they use position descriptions to determine qualifications.

RTC has not developed and implemented standards to evaluate the qualifications of applicants for positions requiring appraisal expertise.

GAO'S COMPOSITE CRITERIA—EDUCATION

* College degree or equivalent work experience
* 7 basic appraisal courses

* Average 20 CPE hours annually

GAO'S Composite Criteria Education

RTC's extensive and varied real estate holdings, their importance and complexity, the dynamic changes in the current real estate market, and appraisal certification reforms required by the Financial Institutions Reform, Recover, and Enforcement Act of 1989 (FIRREA), as amended, call for a high level of both general and real estate specific education. The reforms are to be achieved by state certifying offices by January 1, 1993; 24 states have already implemented these reforms. We believe that RTC's appraisers should have a college education or equivalent experience, as well as have taken specific appraisal courses. They should also exhibit a CPE pattern so they can adjust to the industry's new techniques, methods, and environment. Specifically, RTC appraisers should have the following:

-A degree from a 4-year college or university, preferably in finance, economics, and/or real estate (or, alternatively, qualifying appraisal experience) and professional courses, seminars, and training demonstrating knowledge and skills equal to peers who are college graduates. A requirement for a college level degree is similar to OPM's requirement, and is widely accepted for those in the appraisal industry.

-Credit for completing seven basic courses that address topics, such as appraisal principles and techniques, appraisal applications, capitalization theory and methods, report writing, and appraisal standards. This requirement is similar to that of the Appraisal Institute for its highest level professional designation. Some federal agencies require at least four courses. These courses, or their equivalent, are widely available and are generally considered the minimum qualifiers for the industry appraiser and review appraiser positions.

-Evidence of CPE in the appraisal field with a minimum average of 20 hours annually. Rapid changes within the last 5 years, such as the FIRREA licensing requirements, dictate the need for skill upgrades. The Appraisal Institute and other designation-conferring professional appraisal organizations, as well as federal agencies, require CPE training. Some federal agencies require up to 40 hours annually.

We believe the seven basic courses are necessary for RTC's appraisers, even though the Appraisal Foundation and federal agencies require less. The higher skill levels are needed for RTC's multifaceted appraisal work. The added course work, such as advanced capitalization theory and methods, is usually required for private sector appraisers involved with more complex real estate appraisals that are comparable to RTC's.

GAO's Composite Criteria Experience

* 5 years of qualifying experience
* Progressively more advanced and diversified experience

GAO'S COMPOSITE CRITERIA—EXPERIENCE

We believe that RTC appraisers need progressively more advanced and diverse appraisal experience in conducting appraisals and in reviewing other appraisal work. Specifically, we believe RTC appraisers should have the following:

-A minimum of 5 years of qualifying real estate valuation, real estate appraisal review activities, or a combination thereof. "Qualifying experience" is work for which the individual is the principal appraiser or reviewer. In content, this work exhibits the appraiser's ability to understand and apply real estate concepts and appraisal methodology. "Advanced experience" would include using the more complex methodologies, such as the capitalization method and discounted income analyses, on more complex properties that would include office complexes, hotels, and shopping malls. "Diverse experience" calls for appraising a variety of property types—residential, commercial, and vacant land. OPM experience for a grade 14 appraiser.

-Although management, supervision, or collateral real estate activities are desirable and should be considered, they should not be substituted for qualifying valuation or review experience. Many large private sector appraisal organizations call for their appraisers to develop "hands-on" experience in actually doing appraisals and then writing up the reports.

Industry experience standards require professional judgment in determining whether experience meets the Appraisal Foundation's Uniform Standards of Professional Appraisal Practice. These standards address the (1) quality of work performed, (2) types of reports written, (3) degree of responsibility required, and (4) the variety of properties appraised. These generally accepted standards of appraisal practice apply to both in-house review appraisers as well as contract appraisers and are recognized throughout the United States. RTC's review appraisers, like all other appraisers, must observe these standards to keep their minimum, level of professional practice.

The experience data needed to assess whether the job applicant meets the above criteria require detailed information about the applicant's former work. This information, in many cases, is not now included in the appraiser's job applications. Thus, more data should be requested and standards established so that RTC can make consistent decisions. Without such data, hiring decisions are even more complex.

GAO's ASSESSMENT CATEGORIES

* Qualified

* Probably qualified
* Questionable
* Probably underqualified
* Underqualified

GAO's Assessment Categories

The five classifications we used in our assessment of RTC appraisers were as follows:

1. Qualified—Individual clearly meets the composite criteria.
2. Probably qualified—Information available does not clearly show that individual is qualified, but weight of information supports that this assessment is probable.
3. Questionable—Individual has many factors that could support a qualified assessment, but is apparently deficient in significant composite criteria areas.
4. Probably underqualified—Information available does not clearly show individual is underqualified, but weight of information supports that such an assessment is probable.
5. Underqualified—Individual clearly does not meet composite criteria.

The appraisers assessed as qualified or probably qualified are those who met our composite criteria. In contrast, the three lower categories (questionable, probably underqualified, and underqualified) identify appraisers who did not meet these criteria. In appendix II we provide examples of qualified, questionable, and underqualified appraisers.

GAO's ASSESSMENT RESULTS

* 31 percent met overall qualification criteria
* 53 percent met education criteria
* 71 percent met general experience criteria
* 25 percent met appraisal work experience criteria

GAO's Assessment Results

As shown in figure I.1, of the 51 review appraisers we assessed, 16 (31 percent) met the composite criteria and 35 (69) percent) did not appear to meet the criteria. While most of these latter appraisers met the education and general work experience criteria, they generally did not have enough appraisal experience.

The number of appraisers meeting our composite criteria varied by region and CFP. The Southwest Region had the best overall percentage (50 percent—5 of 10 appraisers). In the other three regions about 28 percent of their appraisers met our criteria. Costa Mesa had the highest percentage meeting our criteria (80 percent) among the CFO's, followed by Dallas (75 percent) and Chicago (67 percent). Five CFOs did not have any appraisers who met the composite criteria.

Education Assessment

Overall, 27 appraisers (53 percent) met our composite education criteria. From our review of the job applications, we found that 45 appraisers (88 percent) had a college degree, 22 appraisers (43 percent) took all seven basic appraisal courses, and 10 (20 percent) met the CPE criteria. The six nongraduates also had not taken many appraisal courses or CPE classes. Only two of these six had taken more than two basic appraisal courses.

The number of appraisers meeting our education composite criteria also varied by region and CFO. The North Central Region had the lowest percentage meeting the criteria, but also had one of the four CFOs (Chicago) where all the appraisers met the criteria. The other CFOs were all the appraisers met the education criteria were Tampa, Houston, and New Jersey. Three CFOs did not have any appraisers meeting the education criteria.

Twenty-four appraisers did not meet the education part of the composite criteria because they did not have enough basic appraisal courses and CPEs. Forty-six appraisers (90 percent) took some, but not all, of the seven basic appraisal courses. Five appraisers (10 percent) said they had not taken any appraisal courses. Although we believe these courses are critical for appraisers, other courses are available. Twenty nine appraisers (57 percent) said they took one to eight other appraisal-related offerings.

Only 11 appraisers (22 percent) had taken the average 20 CPE hours annually during the last 5 years. Of these 11, 2 had taken at least five seminars. Seminars generally involve 3.5 to 17 hours of course instruction. Twelve appraisers (24 percent) specified that they did not take any CPE courses.

General Experience Assessment

Overall, 36 appraisers (71 percent) met the general experience criteria. Job applications showed that 45 appraisers (89 percent) had at least 5 years of appraisal-related experience. General experience again varied by region and CFO. In three of four regions at least 70 percent of the appraisers met the general experience criteria. All appraisers at four CFOs (Kansas City, Chicago, Baton Rouge, and New Jersey) met the criteria.

Appraisal Experience Assessment

Few appraisers met the appraisal experience part of the composite criteria. Thirteen appraisers (25 percent) met the criteria. Appraisal experience also varied by region and CFO. Cost Mesa (80 percent) and Dallas (75 percent) had the highest percentages of appraisers meeting appraisal experience criteria among the CFOs. Eight CFOs had no appraisers with experience meeting the appraisal experience criteria.

RTC Comments

RTC officials, after reviewing this briefing report, expressed concern about our calculated high rate of underqualified appraisers and the methodology used to develop the assessment rankings.

Officials expressed concern that only one GAO appraiser consultant did the assessments, rather than several appraisal experts, and that we had not gathered more information on the appraisers' qualifications. We believe our assessment methodology is strong enough to demonstrate RTC has serious weaknesses, and must act immediately. We agree a stronger methodology using several appraisers and more comprehensive information may have been useful. However, we do not believe this approach would have changed the results significantly. RTC may wish to use such an approach in making its own recommended assessment.

Comments Sr. Appraisers and Standards Committee

* Acknowledged having weak appraisers
* Close supervision needed
* RTC not supporting training needs
* Some CFOs have limited capability
* Standards being considered

COMMENTS—SENIOR APPRAISERS AND STANDARDS COMMITTEE

Several current and previous senior appraisers acknowledged that some of the appraisers they supervise were not, in their opinion, qualified to carry out their duties. Some also stated that close supervision minimized the risks associated with using underqualified appraisers. These senior appraisers expressed concern that training budget limitations were hampering their ability to train those appraisers who need more education or experience. They also expressed concern about what was happening at those CFOs where no qualified senior appraiser was available to supervise the less qualified appraisers.

The senior appraisers were receptive to our suggestions that (1) a chief appraiser was needed to manage the appraisal program, (2) hiring criteria were needed, and (3) more information about educational and appraisal experience were needed from applicants.

Other officials told us that RTC is moving to improve its' appraisal program. Seven task force study groups are evaluating appraisal issues including the needs for better appraiser job descriptions and improved training.

In February 1992, we discussed our composite criteria with the Standards Committee appraiser qualification's task force. Task force members are considering more detailed qualifications for RTC appraisers. The task force chair told us that the group's initial deliberations resulted in education qualification criteria similar to our composite criteria. The task force supports the college degree (or equivalent experience), the same number of CPE hours, and the equivalent of seven courses for the senior review appraisers. The group believes, however, that only five to six courses were needed for the grade 14 appraisers. The task force is also considering a 7 to 10-year experience requirement, and that the work be diverse and increasingly sophisticated. This requirement would be more rigorous than GAO's composite experience criteria.

CONCLUSIONS

* Too many underqualified appraisers
* Chief appraiser needed
* Hiring decisions need improvement
* Need selection criteria
* More applicant information

To be successful, RTC's appraisal program must have qualified people who select and review contract appraisal work and help set appraisal policy. Our review shows that, although RTC has some highly qualified appraisers, 69 percent of its' review appraisers appear to be underqualified for their jobs based on GAO's composite education and experience criteria.

RTC does not have a chief appraiser to set appraisal policies and appraiser qualification and hiring criteria, and to evaluate appraiser performance. We believe this lack led to the current number of underqualified personnel in review appraiser positions.

Also, RTC does not require applicants to submit enough supporting data on education and experience with their job application to enable determination of whether applicants are qualified to fill review appraiser positions. More data about the applicants' educational background and prior appraisal related experience would help RTC identify qualified applicants to fill openings.

Recommendations

* Hire senior executive level chief appraiser
* Assess current qualifications of review appraisers
* Rapidly upgrade capabilities
* Develop hiring criteria
* Require more detailed applicant information

RECOMMENDATIONS

To improve the appraisal program, we are recommending the RTC

- hire a senior executive level chief appraiser to manage and assess the appraisal program's execution,
- assess the appraisal skills and capabilities of the current review appraiser staff,
- upgrade the skills and capabilities of any underqualified review appraisers as rapidly as feasible,
- develop and implement detailed qualification standards and hiring criteria to ensure that qualified personnel are hired, and
- require more complete data from applicants to support their appraisal-related educational background and experience.

APPENDIX II
EXAMPLES OF QUALIFIED, QUESTIONABLE, AND UNDERQUALIFIED ASSESSMENTS

EXAMPLE OF QUALIFIED APPRAISER

The appraiser met the education, general experience, and appraisal experience composite criteria. The appraiser had served as an advanced appraisal course instructor, which shows that the appraiser was well-versed in all types and phases of appraisal work. The appraiser's diversity and level of work experience showed capability.

The appraiser had a bachelor's degree in mathematics. The appraiser only listed two basic appraisal courses on the application but had a Member, Appraisal Institute (MAI); designation. This designation indicates that the appraiser had attended the appraisal courses required by the Institute. While personnel records do not indicate that 20 CPEs had been earned, the appraiser had taught all courses offered by the American Institute of Real Estate Appraisers and the Society of Real Estate Appraisers.

Prior to RTC employment, the appraiser's career spanned 28 years. The appraiser was self-employed for about 23 years and served as president, salesperson, appraiser, consultant, and supervisor. During the period when not self-employed, the appraiser worked 2 years for a nationally known firm as the regional manager of its real estate advisory group. In this capacity, the appraiser generated work, completed assignments, and supervised other appraisers.

The appraiser also worked for about 3 years for a real estate research firm. There, the appraiser served as a senior vice president and supervised appraisers both locally and throughout the country. The appraiser also was responsible for the appraisal's quality control. In this capacity, the appraiser established appraisal conformance standards to maintain product credibility and professionalism.

EXAMPLE OF QUESTIONABLE APPRAISER

The appraiser met the educational and general experience composite criteria. However, the appraiser's appraisal related experience probably did not meet the criteria.

The appraiser received a master's degree in economics and finance in 1990, had a senior residential appraisal designation, and was an MAI candidate. In addition, the appraiser attended 600 hours of appraisal education offerings over the past 6 years.

The appraiser held several positions in private industry and one with RTC before becoming senior appraiser. Even though the appraiser did some appraisals and reviewed reports, the background information shows that the appraiser's main function was as a manager. The appraiser worked about 6 years in the appraisal industry. While attending college, the appraiser worked 1 year as a real estate appraiser, then joined an appraisal firm at a staff level and was later promoted to appraisal manager. For 3 years, the appraiser was responsible for the residential appraisal department. The appraiser was employed for about 2 years at a bank as the assistant vice president and chief appraiser. In this position, the appraiser established an appraisal department, monitored contract appraisers, and coordinated the review of appraisal reports. The appraiser spent 6 months as a commercial real estate consultant/appraiser doing consulting for numerous clients, preparing appraisal and reviewing appraisal reports, and serving as an expert witness. The appraiser spent 2 months as a CFP contract department head. The appraiser set up and managed the contract department that oversaw the contract process and supervised department personnel.

Except for the 1-year period early in the appraiser's career and again while at the private firm for 6 months before RTC employment, the appraiser's experience time does not conform to the criteria. Rather, the appraiser's employment experience was mainly in managerial position. More qualifying work experience or additional information to enable a better assessment could place the appraiser into the qualified category.

EXAMPLE OF UNDERQUALIFIED APPRAISER

The appraiser's educational background was weak, and there was no evidence of qualifying work experience. Education classification was probably not qualified. General experience classification was questionable, and the appraisal experience classification was not qualified.

The appraiser did not have a college degree and took only one appraisal course mentioned in the evaluation criteria; however, the appraiser did attend six appraisal-related courses from 1978 through 1989. The content of these offerings appeared to be "light" and apparently did not include any appraisal examinations. The appraiser was a member of a professional association, but no professional appraisal designation was claimed.

The application had no evidence that the appraiser did work of a sophisticated or diverse nature. The appraiser worked 12 years as a city appraiser, and spent about 11 years as a residential land property appraiser. The appraiser also did appraisals for residential construction and revaluation of existing residential properties. The appraiser was promoted to the commercial property appraiser position and served 18 months in this capacity before coming to RTC.

RELATED GAO PRODUCTS

Land Exchange: Phoenix and Collier Reach Agreement of Indian School Property (GAO/GGD-92-42, Feb. 10, 1992).

Federal Home Loan Mortgage Corporation: Abuses in Multifamily Program Increase Exposure to Financial Losses (GAO/RCED-92-6, Oct. 7, 1992).

Land Exchange: Phoenix Indian School Development Plan Adversely Affects Property Value (GAO/GGD-91-111, July 25, 1991).

Property Disposition: Information on Federal Single-Family Properties (GAO/RCED-91-69, Mar. 29, 1992).

Navy Office Space: Cost Estimate for Consolidating the Naval Systems Commands May Be High (GAO/GGD-91-61, Mar. 8, 1991).

Facilities Location Policy: GSA Should Propose a More Consistent and Businesslike Approach (GAO/GGD-90-109, Sept. 28, 1990).

Conflicting Values for Land Near the Columbia Hospital for Women (GAO/T-GGD-90-39, May 23, 1990).

Federal Timber Sales: Process for Appraising Timber Offered for Sale Needs to Be Improved (GAO/RCED-90-135, Dec. 11, 1989).

Federal Real Property: Conflicting Appraisals of Land Near Columbia Hospital for Women (GAO/GGD-90-15, Dec. 11, 1989).

Federal Real Property: Appraisal of Land to Be Sold to Columbia Hospital for Women (GAO/GGD-89-46, Mar. 10, 1989).

Denver Post Office: Estimate of Fair Market Value (GAO/GGD-88-51, Mar. 11, 1988).

Land Exchange: New Appraisals of Interior's Collier Proposal Would Not Resolve Issues (GAO/GGD-88-85, May 11, 1988).

Internal Controls: Weaknesses in HUD's Single Family Housing Appraisal Program (GAO/RCED-87-165, Sept. 30, 1987).

Federal Land Acquisition: Land Exchange Process Working But Can Be Improved (CAO/RCED-87-9, Feb. 5, 1987).

(247035)

APPENDIX III

MAJOR CONTRIBUTORS TO THIS BRIEFING REPORT

GENERAL GOVERNMENT, DIVISION, WASHINGTON, D.C.

Eugene M. Smith, Program Review Analyst

John D. Dorchester, Jr., MAI, Consultant

KANSAS CITY REGIONAL OFFICE

Jerry W. Pennington, Regional Management Representative

David R. Solenberger, Evaluator-in-Charge

Yong Meador, Evaluator

Rose M. Dorlac, Evaluator

Ruth Anne Decker, Evaluator

EVIDENCE 3

VOL. 137
WASHINGTON, WEDNESDAY, SEPTEMBER 25, 1991
NO. 134

CONGRESSIONAL RECORD

PROEEDINGS AND DEBATES OF
THE 102D CONGRESS, FIRST SESSION
ARIZONA'S SUPERINTENDENT OF BANKS
SPEAKS OUT

Mr. DeConcini. Mr. President, in June, Arizona's superintendent of banks, William H. Rivoir testified before the Resolution Trust Corporation's regional advisory board for region 6. What he had to say to the members of the advisory boards is instructive and useful. It is also very frightening.

Mr. Rivoir's 15 page statement is illuminating; I encourage my colleagues to read it and I ask that his entire statement be included in the RECORD at the end of my remarks.

Mr. Rivoir's statement opens as asserting that "the RTC's basic design and virtually all of the policies and procedures that have emanated from it during its' relatively short life, have only one truly underlying purpose—to shift blame." He goes onto say that "the RTC has reacted...by creating an enormous bureaucracy that is designed to ensure that it and its personnel never make a decision for which they could be held responsible." He concludes that this situation is serious. "It is destroying our local real estate market, it is shrinking our property tax base, it is hindering the bonding ability of local jurisdictions, and more to the point, it is causing RTC to accomplish exactly the opposite of its stated goals...."

I am not an expert on the RTC, Mr. President, but Mr. Rivoir is an expert. I hope my colleagues, especially those on the House and Senate Banking Committees, will consider what he has to say. This statement should be must reading for anyone concerned about the RTC.

The statement follows:

Statement of:
William H. Rivoir II
Superintendent of Banks
State of Arizona

Mr. Chairman, Members of the Board, I appear before you today in the unenviable position of having to bring you bad news. Before I give it to you, however, I want you to remember that I am just the messenger. And no matter how emotionally satisfying it sometimes may be to lop off the head of the messenger, such an action will not eliminate the underlying problems that I am about to report on.

In addition, I want you to be assured that in compiling this testimony, I have personally investigated RTC's operations here in Arizona by talking with a wide range of market participants—Realtors, appraisers, investors, developers, syndicators, accountants, and lawyers. Some of these participants negotiate with or litigate against the RTC, and some work and negotiate for, or litigate on behalf of, the RTC.

Finally, I want to solicit your assistance as you listen to my testimony today. It is not my intention to give offense, but it will be difficult to avoid, because I have some very direct things to say.

They will probably be particularly hard for the RTC personnel present today to listen to, so perhaps I should emphasize something important at the start.

My major complaints against the RTC are structural in nature, but they manifest themselves through the actions of people. Therefore, some of my testimony will necessarily be cast in terms of actions by RTC personnel. But I do not want to criticize the individual RTC employee. As I have said on previous occasions, the RTC has many competent and qualified employees who have the capability of doing a good job. It is not the necessarily the employee, that is at fault. With this as a preface, let me move to the substance of my testimony.

The overwhelming and consistent response from the parties I talked with is that the RTC process in Arizona is going poorly, and its' ill effects are becoming more serious and widespread every day. The situation is so bad that I do not exaggerate when I say that the RTC's operations here are illegal, immoral, wasteful and downright stupid. Even worse, the problem lies at the very core of the RTC and it will take a complete overhaul of the system to rectify it. There are no quick or easy fixes.

Let me start with the fundamental problem. The RTC's basic design, and virtually all of the policies and procedures that have emanated from it during its' relatively short life, have only one true underlying purpose—to shift blame. Congress and the previous administration created the savings and loan debacle, and they gave RTC the job of cleaning it up. This leaves the RTC to take the blame.

The RTC has reacted to this political reality by creating an enormous bureaucracy that is designed to ensure that it and its' personnel never make a decision for which they could be held responsible. There is a policy or a procedure at every step in the process that requires either a mechanical application or a formula or the shifting the decision to someone outside of the RTC. The result has been indecision on so massive a scale that words are inadequate to describe it.

This situation is serious. It is destroying our local real estate market, it is shrinking our property tax base, it is hindering the bonding ability of local jurisdictions, and, more to the point, it is causing the RTC to accomplish exactly the opposite of its stated goals, which are to manage the acquisition of assets from failed savings and loans and to dispose of those assets with the highest possible net recovery for the government and the taxpayer. Instead, the RTC is not managing anything, and it is squandering tens of millions of dollars that should be going to taxpayers.

These are, to put it mildly, strong charges. Now let me back them up. Let's start with asset dispositions.

Currently, the RTC is using two approaches to get rid of the assets it is forced to take back from failed savings and loans. They are (1) sales by private asset managers—the SAMDA program and (2) direct sales by the RTC. I will discuss the SAMDA program first, because it is the centerpiece of the RTC's efforts to utilize the private sector to help dispose of these assets.

Simply stated, the SAMDA program is a bust and should be junked immediately. Instead, the RTC should accelerate its bulk sales program. The assets the RTC owns must be totally free of the government as soon as possible. This is because, despite the high expectations and laudable intentions of using the private sector to dispose of assets in an efficient fashion, the SAMDA program has simply created another unnecessary layer of bureaucracy.

In implementing the SAMDA program, the RTC has held back too much decision making power from the asset managers, while at the same time saddling them with unbelievable paperwork requirements. Asset managers start by wasting the first 90 days of their contract preparing lengthy Asset Management Disposition Plans, known as AMDP, for each asset under their management. They have to follow up with one weekly report, 12 different monthly reports, and three different quarterly reports. There is no time left to actually manage the asset.

In addition, asset managers are apparently picked for every reason expect competence and knowledge of the local market. National companies, many of which have highly knowledgeable and competent local offices, can only be listed in the RTC's data base in one location. This means that lists of eligible contractors for Phoenix will not list any companies who may happen to have their names in the Dallas or Atlanta computers. Also, competent local companies are virtually ignored. The result in the contracts are going to out of town companies.

The RTC's almost total refusal to hire anyone who actually knows anything about the market into which they are to sell assets has become comical. There have been instances where newly appointed out of town assets managers have come to take over portfolios of properties in Arizona and have had to ask where the city of Tucson is in relation to Phoenix, or where downtown Phoenix is. How can these people be knowledgeable enough about our market to manage and sell property here.

Finally, the estimated recovery values in the SAMDA contracts have been set so long ago and at such unrealistic prices that managers have an extremely strong disincentive to sell the properties. Instead, the only economically feasible action is to hold properties forever, receive the management fee, and not take on any more money losing work for the RTC. In addition, asset managers are left with little guidance or standardization for their work. The RTC does not provide asset managers with standardized forms for purchase and sale agreements, letters of intent, warranty deeds, limited representations and warranties, property management agreements, brokerage listing forms, office building leases, or triple net retail leases.

There is an alternative, however, for the asset manager, and that is to appeal the ERV. And how is that done? The asset manager gets to hire an appraiser to provide a new value. But guess what. That puts the asset manager in exactly the same position that the developers and speculators were vis a vis the savings and loans during the last decade. In other words, there's a big conflict of interest here. If an asset manager wants to sell property quickly, it pushes for an unrealistically low value. If it wants to manage the property for a long time, it pushes for an unrealistically high value.

The asset managers accomplish this by using appraisers who are chosen solely on the basis of lowest price. Asset managers are also hiring totally unqualified personnel to engage appraisers. These personnel don't have any idea what goes into a proper appraisal. Hence, bids for appraisals can have a differential of over 300 percent, ranging from fly by night companies on the low end to reputable firms at the higher end. And, as I said before, the lowest cost always wins. Quality is not even considered.

However, despite all this failure in the SAMDA program, the RTC has accomplished it underlying goals. First, it has shifted blame for the failure away from the RTC and onto the asset manager. Second, because of all the reports it requires, it can deflect charges of inaction because it has created a huge paper trail that offers well documented process as a substitute for real progress. This substitution of paperwork for results is a continuing theme throughout all areas of RTC's asset disposition operations.

The other disposition method used by RTC is direct sales out of the conservatorships and receiverships. This program is also plagued by major structural problems. Once again, the major flaw is that no one at the RTC will make a decision, RTC personnel spend more time looking for ways that a deal won't work, than in finding ways in which it will work. And when they run out of excuses and are forced to agree to a sale, no one will approve the deal to get it closed. That is different from saying that RTC local personnel don't have adequate delegated authority. In many instances, they do. They just won't use it.

This consistent indecision manifested by the RTC has produced a continuing lack of responsiveness. It takes forever to get a decision made, and when it is made, it is overruled later, or it turns out either that the person who made it is reassigned, or the asset is reassigned, or the person never had the authority to decide in the first place. In fairness, I must add that some market participants feel that the RTC's responsiveness has improved, but they are either dealing in residential real estate or with a conservatorship. For the rest of the RTC's asset disposition programs, responsiveness remains dismal.

The next issue under asset disposition concerns appraisals. The appraisals the RTC is getting are of very low quality. On one recent appraisal of a multimillion dollar project, the appraiser didn't even bother to contact the borrower who was managing the project to find out the status of the current leases. Then the appraiser just arbitrarily factored in future rent increases which have little hope of being realized. Also, some RTC contracting personnel have made it clear that appraisers must be ordered on the basis of race, sex and price, with price being the most important. The informed judgment of the person hiring the appraiser is explicitly excluded from the process.

In fairness, there are some exceptions to this. However, the process still requires that appraisal contracts, as well as legal work, property management, sales listings, etc. be given out to companies whose names are generated in a random fashion from a list of registered providers. At Southwest Savings, this random generation process consists of putting slips of paper into a shoe box and picking out names like awarding door prizes.

Secondly, the RTC is still a very slow pay, taking up to 120 days to settle its bills. Major reputable appraisal firms will not bid for RTC work because they are undercut by inexperienced firms who are desperate for the work, and they won't wait 120 days for payment. Experienced RTC personnel are frustrated by having to lower their standards for the quality of appraisal work they must accept. They know they are getting bad work, but they are powerless to contravene policy in order to get quality appraisals.

Finally, the RTC does not make the appraiser's life easy. RTC cannot provide its' own appraisers with rent rolls, legal descriptions of the property, a list of recent offers, or listing information and offers on similar RTC property. Frankly, RTC should not even order an appraisal until it has the standard information available. Also, if it must bid out an appraisal without the information available, it should so inform the potential bidders. Otherwise a $2,000 bid could turn out to be a $10,000 job, and the result will be that the appraiser cannot afford to do a good appraisal.

Next, the RTC should substantially reduce the use of brokers' opinions. In one case, the RTC is paying $3,500 each for simple brokers' opinions on a package of mini-warehouses. Not only is this too much to pay, brokers' opinions are not independent, estimates of value. Instead, they are opinions designed to facilitate a sale. A sale that might not be in the RTC's best interests. Frankly, brokers are telling the RTC what they want to hear; that the appraisal is much too high and that the property should be sold for much less. In other words, the broker wants his commission. The

RTC should not rely on these parties whose interests conflict with the RTC's interests.

Of course, many people complain that appraisals take too long, but there is a collateral issue here that has received very little notice so far. That issue is environmental liability. Every piece of commercial property that the RTC wants to sell needs an environmental study. Once these studies are complete they go to the Phoenix office's environmental section for approval.

This is where the bottleneck lies. Unless it is a major property, or a major environmental problem, the environmental study does not get approved. It's a simple lack of staff. And if the environmental study doesn't get approved, then the appraisal can't be completed. Hence, the property can't be sold. This backlog affects even clean sites, those where no environmental problem exists. They are all stacked up at the Phoenix office. This problem also affects loan workouts, which I will discuss below. The workout can't proceed because the appraisal can't be completed without an approved environmental study.

The next issue concerns the terms of a property sale. First of all, the RTC standard purchase form and sale contract is not a contract at all. It is totally illusory. It specifically states that the RTC has absolutely no duty to live up to its part of the contract. And when RTC does default, it does so with impunity. Under the contract, no damages can be assessed against RTC, regardless of how much damage its' actions may have caused. And don't be misled. The RTC is causing damage. And even if that exculpatory language in the contract could be overcome, it doesn't matter. Any judgment against an RTC receivership would be so far down the payment priority list, that it would never get paid, RTC employers know this and they exploit it.

The RTC feels no compunction whatsoever about breaking

deals in escrow simply because somebody else comes along and offers a dollar more. This practice is not only reprehensible, it is stupid. Knowledgeable buyers will not put up with this type of practice, and they will cease doing business with the RTC. Also, the same RTC contract allows the RTC to break the deal if it suddenly decides that it doesn't like you. It's called the "Identity of Purchaser" section. It allows absolute discretion in the rejecting a buyer for any reason. Once again, the contract specifically prohibits any liability on the RTC's part for any damages it causes.

Next, when RTC sells personal property along with realty, it gives a quit claim bill of sale. In other words, it sells you the personal property, takes your money, and then won't tell you whether it actually owned what it just sold. They buyer is totally exposed. Next, the RTC requires the buyer of income property to collect back rent owed and pay it to the RTC. This means that the buyer might have to refuse to accept the rent currently due to it in order to apply any payments received to RTC. Instead, if there are back rent due, the RTC should preserve its claims and pursue them itself.

Next, there are no provisions for proration of personal property tax. Next, there are no provisions for turning over deposits and prepaid rents, etc. Next, if there is a loss during escrow, the buyer can cancel the contract if it is a "substantial loss." But if it is less than a substantial loss, then the buyer must close at the full purchase price, with RTC assigning over all rights to insurance proceeds. But here's the catch—RTC self insures. There are no insurance proceeds. So RTC just forces you to close at full price and you get stuck with the loss, despite the clear language of the contract that RTC assumes all such risks and liabilities. For all these reasons, this purchase agreement is worthless, and knowledgeable buyers will not deal in this fashion.

The next issue is the intrusion into the asset disposition process of political concerns, both real and perceived. No one wants to force the RTC to negotiate with people who were engaged in fraudulent activities. But the RTC has developed a paranoia about dealing with anyone who ever had anything to do with a property. In addition, the RTC Phoenix office has wrongly assumed the role of Lord High Executioner.

Instead of concentrating on how to obtain the highest net recovery on a particular asset, local RTC personnel are convinced that they have some sort of divine patriotic duty to reek moral retribution on everyone who was ever associated with a savings and loan, even an innocent borrower. The head of the Phoenix office and his subordinates told me this directly. They believe they must enforce moral obligations (as they see fit to define those obligations) even where there exists absolutely no legal obligation. Again, in fairness, I must point out that Mr. Koopmans was also present at the meeting and to his credit, he recognized that this was an inappropriate posture for the RTC to take. But, unfortunately, nothing has changed.

The RTC must relax its conflict of interest standards and work with knowledgeable local players to get the highest net recovery. Unless there was fraud, don't blackball someone who caused a loss to the fund. He or she is mostly just another victim of federal tax and regulatory policy. Unfortunately, the RTC still annihilates everyone in its unnecessary bankruptcies and deliberately destroying the lives and businesses of people whose only sin is that they borrowed from a savings and loan.

Why does the RTC do this? Two reasons. First, as stated above, because of their paranoia about perceived political ramifications, they insist on eliminating any chance that they could be accused of dealing with anyone, who was even remotely involved in the savings and loan debacle, even as an innocent borrower. Second, and this goes back to that continuing theme I mentioned before, by litigating to the ninth degree, RTC personnel can once again avoid having to make a rational business judgment for which they can be called to account. Now, the person to blame for all the decisions is the lawyer. He or she recommended all the litigation, for which, not coincidentally, they are paid handsomely from the government's bottomless trough. Also, RTC personnel can once again substitute documented process (such as foreclosure dates, deficiency judgment dates, and bankruptcy dates) to no real progress.

It does not matter that the RTC now has even more stigmatized RTC property for which it must pay 18 to 20% a year in carrying costs. It does not matter that the borrower might have been willing and able to salvage the deal through renegotiation—a renegotiation which would have avoided RTC holding costs, management costs, appraisal fees, environmental assessment fees, environmental liabilities, sales commissions, etc. It does not matter that the money which the borrower might have paid in as a part of a renegotiation has now been spent on lawyers. It does not matter that yet another market player is in bankruptcy.

What matters is that RTC personnel never had to go out on a limb and make a reasonable business decision. What matters is that RTC personnel have shifted the blame for no recovery onto the lawyers and then onto the bankruptcy court. What matters is that RTC personnel shifted the blame to someone else, and in the process they created a documented paper trail to pretend that they achieved a worthwhile result.

The next thing the RTC is paranoid about is letting anyone make a profit from an RTC deal. RTC personnel have said so directly to potential buyers. In one case, RTC was willing to sell a piece of vacant land with two year financing. But a part of the deal was that the buyer could neither develop nor sell the land during the two years. Why? RTC said explicitly that they were afraid that the buyer would make a profit. Again, this is ridiculous and self-defeating. The only reason anyone will think of buying RTC properties is to make a profit. It's called capitalism.

Next, even if you strike a deal with the RTC, you have to worry about closing. Example #1. Buyer makes a bid for the property and is told he must pay cash. He goes out and raises the cash. He calls the RTC every day to make sure that the property is still available and is assured that it is. When he arrives with the cash, a new person is in charge of the file, and informs him that the property has been placed in escrow with someone else several weeks earlier. Example #2. Local RTC office puts a property in escrow. Buyer spends money for due diligence, etc. Then unbeknownst to the local RTC office, the regional office sells the property to someone else. Example #3. Buyer has an RTC property in escrow on a seller financing deal. Before closing, but after paying substantial due diligence costs, a new buyer offers a lower price but pays cash. RTC breaks the escrow and sells to new buyer. I don't think further comment is necessary on these examples.

Another aspect of the asset disposition process that must be junked is the arbitrary implementation of the "exposure to the market" concept. While it is certainly a good idea in many instances to ensure that a property is adequately exposed to the market (in order to obtain the highest price), the RTC is using this concept as yet another excuse to not make a decision. We are aware of a number of instances where RTC will refuse to sell property, or even negotiate with a potential buyer, without arbitrarily delaying the entire process for endless months in order to "expose the property to the market."

Many of the RTC's properties are not particularly attractive, and the only reasonable expectation of sale is to the person who contacted the RTC—often because they have some unique interest or position that makes this property attractive to them. RTC should follow the oldest of clinches and recognize that a bird in a hand is worth two in the bush. But instead of negotiating a sale with the prospective buyer at a price which would require the RTC to make a business judgment about what constitutes a reasonable price, the RTC defaults on its' responsibilities and "exposes the property to the market." Most times, the market ignores the property, and when the RTC returns to the first potential buyer, that person is either gone or offers less because of the market's response. In this way, RTC is losing millions of dollars through foolish consistency.

Next, when an offer is rejected by the RTC, that's all it does. It says "your offer is rejected. Good-bye." No reasons, no counter-offers, nothing. How does a buyer respond to such a message. First, with bewildered expletives. Second, by never dealing with the RTC again.

The next item is the RTC's time table for lowering prices to meet the market. This policy must be eliminated immediately. The practical effect of this policy is to say to the world: "Don't buy now. This is not the bottom of the market. It will go much, much lower." The well intentioned idea behind this policy was to allow RTC personnel the flexibility to lower prices from potentially unrealistic appraised values down to real market values.

When the first version of this policy was implemented a year ago, we spoke in favor of it. We were wrong. By enforcing a mechanical racketing down, the effect is to turn the policy on its' head. It actually forces the market lower and prevents sales from happening. Incidentally, while I acknowledge that the ostensible purpose of this policy was well intentioned, it is appropriate to point out that, once again, the effect of the policy is to allow RTC personnel to avoid making business judgments for which they could be criticized. If the property doesn't sell, the fault lies with the appraised value which was set, not coincidentally, by someone outside of the RTC. If the RTC drops the price by the stated percentage, the RTC employee is simply effectuating a mechanical application of a policy.

This mark down policy is having and will continue to have an extremely destabilizing effect on a vast amount of real estate. And instability is just not in the RTC's best interests. The only way RTC can ultimately obtain the highest net recovery is to sell into a stabilized market. Somehow, the RTC must convince the market that the bottom is here now.

The way the RTC is to achieve that is to give its' personnel the ability to sell for what they, in their best judgment, believe represents a good deal for the RTC. The amount of money the RTC would probably lose though some bad judgments pales into insignificance in comparison to the money it will continue to lose because it is driving the market down, and because it can't or won't sell in a prompt or orderly fashion.

The inability or refusal to sell was recently illustrated by a case here in Phoenix. Although the asset was unusual, the RTC's handling of the case was typical. The asset in question is a 30 animal and two chariot merry-go-round—perfect metaphor for the RTC. The RTC tried to sell the carousel recently. It got bids from around the country, after nationwide advertising. The RTC wanted $175,000—the highest of 10 bids was $89,000. This response was the market telling the RTC that the appraisal was wrong. But did RTC listen? No. Apparently they feel that the next time it is offered, someone will bid higher. I doubt it.

The point of this one small example is that RTC seems obsessed with trying to recoup value that doesn't exist. It probably never existed, it was just pumped up by the steroids of mid 80's fax policy. The RTC has to face reality and try to recoup what value is actually left to its' assets. When the market tells you what the value is, sell at that value.

The next issue is auctions. In my previous testimony, I praised the RTC for its auction of 65 properties conducted by Grubb & Ellis. I strongly urged that the next auction occur as soon as possible to take advantage of the momentum the first auction established. David Cooke, the Executive Director of the RTC, was kind enough to write me about my previous testimony and in part he said "Your insight into the marketing time of auction events is correct. The next auction in Phoenix should take place quickly."

Four months have already gone by, and no other auction has been held. This is not "quickly" by anyone's definition, and the precious momentum is likely lost. In addition, it is my understanding that only one third of the properties were sold at the auction, and that sales on only another third or so are expected to close this year. This is like repeatedly stepping halfway towards a wall—you never actually get to your goal. At the rate the RTC is taking back new properties, it can't afford to step only part way towards its' goal by leaving a significant portion of an auction's properties unsold. RTC will get further behind with every event.

Next, we should discuss marketing strategies. The RTC is not physically capable of effectively marketing all of its' properties at the same time. Therefore, some properties will have to remain off the market for the time being. RTC should carefully chose certain types of property to keep off the market. Foremost among these is raw land. The holding costs are the least here, and the market is the worst. You simply cannot force the market to buy products it doesn't want, even if you price it ridiculously low. Therefore, much of the raw land inventory of the RTC should be land banked simply to allow the market to absorb it at a sustainable rate and to allow the RTC to concentrate on selling other assets.

There is one major exception to the foregoing advice, however, and that is bulk sales of assets. All RTC assets, including raw land, should be included in bulk sales. It is always better to bet the decision as to disposing of an asset completely into the hands of a private owner acting for his or her own private pecuniary interests.

The last issue I want to discuss under this asset disposition heading is the credit committee system. This process also seems to be a big bottleneck. My information is that only five to seven deals are even presented each week to each receivership's credit committee. Hardly a breakneck pace. What's worse is that only two or three of those cases get approved, so the backlog just gets bigger and bigger. Finally, and this ties in with the overuse of broker's opinions, RTC's own personnel fee that much of the RTC's inventory is simply being given away. The sale personnel strike deals based upon broker's opinions without even bothering to discuss value with their own in-house appraisal department. They then ask the appraisal personnel to rubber stamp the lower value suggested by the broker, and pass it on to the credit committee. This is not the case in the remaining conservatorship, Southwest Savings, but it does hold true for the receiverships. The receiverships could learn a lot from Southwest.

The next issue is loan restructuring. We have harped on this issue over and over again, and we continue to receive the same lip service from the RTC. Unfortunately, we don't see any results. Contrary to the RTC's public position, loan restructurings are not being pursued, and foreclosure is still the first and only resort. Of course, this practice does serve RTC's underlying purposes. RTC can never be criticized for being too easy on a savings and loan "kingpin" if it mindlessly litigates every troubled borrower into submission. But this is ultimately self-defeating for the RTC.

First, as we have stated over and over again, the RTC does not need any more property in its REO portfolio. The RTC should be desperately seeking ways to minimize its use of foreclosure, rather than using it in virtually every case. Again, I recognize that a file that shows trustee sale dates, deficiency suit filing dates, bankruptcy filing dates, etc. presents a superficial impression of progress. But as we have said before, this is false progress. It is progress and not results. The real results are that RTC is forcing out of business the very parties who could most effectively assist it in salvaging problem loans and problem projects. These people are the real estate professionals who are currently in the deal and are willing to work hard to save it, if only the RTC would take a realistic look at what is left to be saved.

When I made the same points at you last meeting, I followed up by meeting directly with the local RTC office on a particular case. A very well respected and reputable local builder took the courageous step of letting me use its' loans from one of the conservatorships as a case study. In preparation for the meeting with the RTC, I met with the developer and reviewed the loans and the status of the property securing them. So that I would not be in the position of having listened only to a borrower's perspective, I also met with senior loan work-out specialists at two of our major local banks. I discussed how they might structure a work-out on these loans if the loans belonged to their bank.

Armed with this information, I met with Mr. Koopmans, Mr. Porter and two of Mr. Porter's associates. After about two hours of what the diplomats call a candid exchange of views, the RTC agreed that the case study was indeed the type of transaction where a negotiated settlement would be in the best interest of the RTC (even though these loans had already been set for foreclosure). They agreed that the types of concessions on both sides that I discussed were the types that they would pursue, and they agreed that they would in fact pursue negotiations with this borrower.

Months have gone by. The RTC has, in fact, had further negotiations with the borrower, but no resolution is in sight. The question I ask is, why not? There has been plenty of time. This case has been given specific prominence by the fact that I brought it to their attention through a personal meeting. They must have known that would follow its' progress to see if the RTC actually lives up to its fine sounding pronouncements. And yet, they have not even been able to renegotiate successfully in this one high profile matter.

This does not augur well for the hundreds of other cases that did not get special attention. RTC must somewhere find strength of will to actually finalize a deal rather than keeping it going around and around and around. This case study should have been negotiated and closed a long time ago. The longer it festers, the worse the result will be to the taxpayer. RTC is shirking its legal duty by its inaction, and this must stop.

On a slightly more detailed level, the RTC should recognize that its' success in realizing recovery on its problem loans is, in most cases, tied inextricably to the current borrower. To make the process work (and by work, I mean obtaining actual recoveries and resolving the outstanding work load. I do not mean creating more meaningless paperwork) the RTC must realize that it has to become partners with the borrower—a defacto joint venture. In other words, the RTC and the borrowers share a great deal—they both have interests in the project that is troubled. They both want the project to succeed so that they both get some money out of it. And they both should realize that the best way to achieve that is to work together, developing mutual goals and strategies.

In context, working together requires several items. First, the RTC must get an accurate idea of what is really left of the value of the project. Forget about those appraisals done in 1986-they're worthless. Also, forget about the difference between the loan amount and the present value. That difference is already lost, and if RTC can't get past harping on this loss, and trying to blame the borrower for it, it will never face the reality of the situation and be able to achieve its statutory goals.

Next, it is clear that each side to these negotiations will start out at different points. That's what negotiations are for. But the point of the negotiations must be to finally strike a deal. Unfortunately, the RTC is not very interested in striking a deal. If it cannot dictate its own unrealistic terms, it takes its' ball and goes home. Like the child that does the same thing at the playground, the RTC is ultimately the loser in this process. It then ends up with more and more property—property which it manages effectively and then sells at a liquidation price.

This method of operation must change. One step in that process would be for each side to disclose the basis for its' position. In other words, each side should disclose its' appraisal, or at least the assumptions and conclusions of the appraisal. Then, after both sides have had the opportunity to comment on the validity of the appraisal factors, the RTC should exercise its own business judgment to reach a negotiated settlement.

Lastly, the RTC must think about how it will divest itself of the pool of restructured loans it will obtain if it begins to do good faith restructurings. We suggest that these restructurings be accomplished with relatively uniform documentation and terms so that these loans can be sold in pools. If the restructuring are accomplished on realistic terms (particularly the new loan amounts), and the RTC otherwise improves its operations so that it stabilizes our real estate market, these loans will become better and better credits, and easier to sell.

The next issue I would like to discuss is property management. Once again, the RTC is shooting itself in the foot by relying on arbitrary policies that eliminate any requirement for the exercise of business judgment. First, RTC will not spend any money to improve its' properties. This is taken to the ridiculous extreme of not even being willing to pay for tenant improvements for tenants who want to rent empty RTC space. Also, RTC will not spend money to enhance value. In one case, a developer asked the RTC for less than $25.00 as its' share to master plan a parcel that belonged to the developer and which was surrounded on two sides by RTC property. As a result, the developer's property has now been master planned alone, and the majority of commercial, retail and multi-family housing will be on the developer's parcel. The probable loss to the RTC, which will now only get R-1-10 zoning, is about $2 million. That's a lot more than being penny wise and pound foolish.

Another important issue is the zoning on RTC land. Nothing is being done to preserve favorable zoning. That is viewed as the buyer's problem. But zoning does not last forever, and once it is gone, it might never be recovered. Neither will the value it conferred.

The final matters I would like to discuss are the RTC's practices regarding litigation. According to its own lawyers, the RTC is endlessly pursuing uncollectable claims, failing to respond to or rejecting reasonable settlement proposals, and pawing off on the lawyers all kinds of non-legal business decisions. The RTC's lawyers have found a perfect client—a client with endless amounts of money who is willing to litigate forever and who exercises no control over its' counsel.

This situation has a number of causes, including the continuing theme of RTC passing decision making responsibility onto non-RTC personnel. But there is also a deeper, and more insidious, cause. We have already talked about how RTC personnel are a law unto themselves, unanswerable to anyone they damage. We have also talked about how the RTC's paranoia about political concerns, and their messianic compulsion to mete out justice, have caused them to reject reasonable settlements and restructuring. They prefer instead to litigate a borrower into submission without regard for the morality, let alone the cost effectiveness, of their actions. But into this mix we must now add the D'Oench, Duhme doctrine. This doctrine has made the RTC invincible, and the RTC has used this power with a vengeance.

Until a very few years ago, D'Oench, Duhme & Co. v. FDIC was an obscure banking law case that had lain essentially fallow for almost 50 years. Decided in 1942, it says that when a regulatory body takes control of a depository institution, it is not bound to honor any claims or defenses unless the factors which created that claim or defense are a part of the official written records of the institution and are part of a transaction which has received official approval of the committee, loan committee or the like. Congress later codified certain applications of that doctrine into 12 W.S.C. 1823(c).

From its beginning in 1989, the RTC has latched onto D'Oench as a weapon of formidable power. The result has been the creation of a bureaucratic agency whose self-concept is rival only by the Internal Revenue Service. The RTC has been abetted in this attitude by its' outside attorneys who are never hesitant to push a procedural advantage to the limits of ethical conduct and sometimes beyond. For whatever reason, the RTC hires and, apparently, rewards those attorneys who are the most difficult to deal with on a reasonable basis.

As an example, in the litigation involving construction of Phoenician Hotel, after two years in state court, with trial coming close, the RTC suddenly removed the case to federal court just when state rules would require RTC to list its' witnesses and exhibits. The subcontractors who really did do the construction work and have legitimate claims for payment, have had their claims bought out for a small percentage of their worth, with taxpayer money providing the funds. The same taxpayer funds have exhausted those subcontractors by two years of intensive state court litigation. The final straw is the moratorium which is then imposed in federal court by the RTC to push the trial date off even further. This is done, not in the interest of justice morality, but solely because the RTC, under D'Oench, etc. has the power to unfairly bludgeon these people into unfavorable settlements. Thus the unchecked excesses of government power have severely harmed innocent citizens simply because it had the power, and the lack of moral character, to do so.

We find ourselves now with a governmental agency intent not upon resolving a bad situation in the manner best for all of this country's citizens, but one focused on punishing all of the "participants" in the S&L disaster, even when those "participants" were, themselves, the victims of the collapse. We find ourselves with a governmental agency not striving to construct a long term solution, but one satisfied with viciously attacking each individual problem with no thought for whether that attack forwards the legitimate goals of the RTC. And we find ourselves with a government agency where its' agents have adopted a rigid moralistic attitude that stifles even rudimentary problem-solving techniques and attitudes.

Government has a duty to treat its citizens fairly. It must self-police since the powers we necessarily grant government are broad. The RTC has breached this covenant with our citizens, and some measure of control and justice must be restored.

Mr. Chairman, I could go on and on, but I believe that the major points have been made. The RTC is violating its own legal mandate by failing to obtain the highest net recovery on the assets it is taking back and by causing serious and unnecessary harm to our local real estate market. The RTC is acting in a morally reprehensible fashion by violating its own contracts and wantonly driving individuals and companies into bankruptcy. The RTC is wasting millions of dollars of taxpayer money on needless litigation, and it is acting stupidly when it ignores zoning issues, when it refuses to pay even modest amounts to significantly enhance the value of its assets, and when it refuses to make any decisions other than default decisions.

Your job, Mr. Chairman and members of the Board, is to make these problems clear to the Oversight Board, that Board, which wrote the Strategic Plan, and which sets the overall policies of the RTC, must take prompt action to see that the policies of the RTC are changed. The policies must be designed so that they encourage real results, rather than elaborate processes. They must be designed to encourage RTC line personnel to make the business decisions of which they are capable, rather than hobbling them with a stifling bureaucracy. They must be designed to ensure that the RTC operates in a just and equitable fashion.

Lastly, Mr. Chairman, I implore you to forcefully contradict the assertion by National Advisory Board Chairman Philip F. Searle in his May 15, 1991 remarks to the Oversight Board. Mr. Searle said that he has heard nothing about any discernible adverse impact on real estate markets arising out of RTC asset sales activities. Tell him that the RTC's activities in Arizona are destroying Arizona's real estate market, and they are destroying the RTC's ability to do its legally mandated job. Mr. Chairman, make sure that Mr. Searles cannot make that same statement again.

Thank you for the opportunity to appear here today, Mr. Chairman. I apologize for the length of my testimony, and I thank you for your indulgence in letting me present it in full.

EVIDENCE 4

CRS ISSUE BRIEF

THE SAVINGS AND LOAN CLEANUP: BACKGROUND AND PROGRESS

Updated September 6, 1991

By: Barbara Miles and Thomas Woodward
Economic Division
Congressional Research*The Library of Congress

CONTENTS

Contributor to this brief: M. Maureen Murphy

SAVINGS AND LOAN CLEANUP: BACKGROUND AND PROGRESS

SUMMARY

The Resolution Trust Corporation (RTC) was set up in August 1989 by the Financial Institutions Reform, Recovery, and Enforcement Act (FIRREA) for the purpose of closing insolvent savings and loan associations, making good on Federal guarantees to the depositors of those institutions, and disposing of the assets taken over in the closures. The taxpayer-funded cost of this "cleanup" is expected eventually to be on the order of $150 billion for "resolving" about 1,000 insolvent thrifts.

The failures precipitating the cleanup and their great expense were due to three interrelated phenomena: first, the maturity risk-borrowing short-term deposits to lend for long-term mortgages—which was the basis for the thrift industry; second, the presence of Federal deposit insurance which removed any incentive for depositor concern over the safety and soundness of individual institutions; and third, the policy of forbearance which allowed failing institutions to continue to operate long after they would have gone out of business except for the Federal deposit guarantees.

Funding for the RTC was initially $50 billion, which was financed through a somewhat circuitous mechanism in order to keep the outlay mostly off-budget and avoid what could have been costly program disruptions for the sake of settling the debt. The result of the low funding, however, has been that the RTC has repeatedly run low on funds, thus impeding the cleanup process. Whenever this happens, the costs go up because the institutions not closed continue to lose money. Funding is needed both for the permanent losses—outlays which are not recovered through sales of assets—and also "working capital." Only loss funds are appropriated. Working capital is used as "up-front" money, to carry the assets taken over until they can be sold and the money recovered. Under a FIRREA formula, the RTC may only borrow up to 85% of the assets it holds for this purpose; the rest must be financed by holding back loss funds.

There are three ways to resolve failed thrifts. The most common is to allow another financial institution to buy it, with most of its good assets. The second most common transfers the deposits to a healthy institution which then becomes the paying agent for the RTC. The third is a simple deposit payout directly from the RTC which takes over all assets.

Assets taken over by the RTC include both financial paper (securities, including "junk bonds," mortgages, and other loans) and real property (land, houses, commercial buildings). There are major marketing, legal, environmental, legal set-aside, and other difficulties in disposing of these assets, which nonetheless are supposed to be sold quickly. By the end of June 1991, the RTC had disposed of $172 billion, but still held $160 billion in total assets. Eventually, about $500 billion in assets are expected to be handled by the RTC.

ISSUE DEFINITION

The Federal Government is currently trying to close hundreds of insolvent savings and loan institutions while honoring the guarantee of deposits it gave to millions of the institutions' customers. The cost of this operation is being born by taxpayers. This taxpayer-funded cleanup of the industry required the periodic authorization of funds as well as continuing attention to the issue of whether the process of closure is carried out in the most timely, least disruptive, and most efficient manner possible.

BACKGROUND AND ANALYSIS

In August 1989, Congress passed the Financial Institutions

Reform, Recovery, and Enforcement Act (FIRREA), the principal component of which was a taxpayer-funded program of savings and loan (S&L or thrift) closures. The institutions at which this "cleanup" effort was aimed were insolvent and held billions of dollars in deposits insured by the Government through the Federal Savings and Loan Insurance Corporation (FSLIC). The cleanup is eventually expected to involve a thousand or more troubled institutions and cost taxpayers on the order of $150 billion. This issue brief explains how the cleanup became necessary, what it was designed to achieve, and how it is progressing.

ORIGINS OF THE PROBLEM

Three phenomena combined to create widespread insolvencies among S&Ls in the 1980s. First, the basis for the industry under Federal and State law was one of accepting short-term deposits from the public and lending for long-term mortgages. This arrangement ensured profits for the industry only if long-term rates exceeded short-term rates, and if rates over time remained fairly steady. When interest rates began their climb from the mid-1960s to the early 1980s, institutions found themselves earning low interest rates on their loans long after they had to start paying high interest rates for their deposits (or else lose the deposits). This movement in interest rates, combined with the structure of the industry, put a severe squeeze on industry earnings, carrying many thrifts into, or to the brink of, insolvency.

Second, the presence of deposit insurance meant that depositors of troubled institutions' had little incentive to withdraw their funds on account of their institutions's poor financial condition. In the absence of insurance, concern on the part of depositors for the safety of their money would have led to massive withdrawals and failure of the institutions. With insurance, the institutions stayed open.

Third, regulators followed a policy of "forbearance" with respect to troubled thrifts, allowing them to operate in insolvent or nearly insolvent conditions. In this way a Government loan guarantee (deposit insurance) kept institutions operating long after the point at which they would have gone out of business in the absence of Government assistance. In short, the industry was being "bailed out."

Combined, these three phenomena were a recipe for large financial losses. Since an insolvent institution has more liabilities than assets, it has no value to the owner unless it can be brought back to solvency. Consequently, the owners and operators of troubled thrifts had nothing to lose by engaging in riskier lending—but had much to gain as such lending brought big earnings and returned the institution to solvency. Depositors, because they were protected from losses by deposit insurance, had nothing to lose from institutions' risky lending either, and were often attracted to such institutions by the high interest rates offered on deposits. The Government, through its policy of forbearance, did not act to constrain risky lending, even though it did stand to lose from such lending practices. Thus, all the incentives worked to encourage risky lending on the part of troubled institutions. This practice generated further losses.

Since deposits are insured, closing down an insolvent institution costs the Government money. Deposits that are guaranteed are worth more than an insolvent institution's assets. Thus, in paying off depositors, or in getting another, healthy institution to take over a troubled thrift, the Government must lay out funds. Throughout the 1980s, the magnitude of the insolvencies in the industry exceeded the resources of the FSLIC.

In 1987, $12 billion was provided through an off-budget recapitalisation of the FSLIC to close down troubled institutions.

The inadequacy of this sum combined with other constraints meant that the closures proceeded too slowly. Losses continued to mount. In late 1988, the FSLIC engaged in a flurry of activity to deal with as many troubled institutions as possible. In doing so, it committed itself to paying sums in the future to purchases of thrifts far in excess of the resources it had available. Many of these arrangements involved further guarantees by the Government, as well as tax benefits to the purchasers. Yet, by the beginning of 1989, many more institutions needed to be dealt with.

FIRREA AND THE CLEANUP

In August 1989, Congress passed FIRREA. While the legislation addressed various aspects of regulation of the industry, it was principally focused on closing down insolvent and other capital-deficient institutions. FSLIC was eliminated and the responsibility of insuring thrifts was given to the Federal Deposit Insurance Corporation (FDIC), the insurer of banks. The actual cleaning up of insolvent institutions was given to the Resolution Trust Corporation (RTC), which was to resolve all thrifts failing between the beginning of 1989 through most of 1992. To administer and honor commitments made in connection with thrifts resolved prior to implementation of the legislation, the FSLIC Resolution Fund was set up.

The Board of Directors of the RTC consists of the Board of Directors of the FDIC, with the chair of the FDIC Board also chairing the RTC Board. Oversight is vested in the RTC Oversight Board, consisting of the Secretary of the Treasury, Secretary of Housing and Urban Development (HUD), the Chairman of the Federal Reserve Board (Fed), and two other members appointed by the President.

Initial financing for the RTC consisted of $50 billion. Under the Administration's original cleanup proposal, this sum was to come from an off-budget financing entity, the Resolution Funding Corporation (REFCORP). REFCORP was to be provided with approximately $6 billion by the Federal Home Loan Banks (previous to FIRREA, the Federal Home Loan Bank System was the regulator of federally chartered thrifts and the parent of FSLIC). With the $6 billion, REFCORP was to buy "zero-coupon" Treasury securities having a face value of $50 billion, maturing in 30 years. Such securities are simply promises to pay a certain sum in the future, bearing no coupon interest, so that they sell at only a fraction of the value they will hold 30 years hence. REFCORP could then turn around and sell $50 billion of its own securities to raise the needed funds. The zeros in the hands of REFCORP acted as a guarantee that the principal on REFCORP's borrowing could be repaid. REFCORP would then pay interest on its' borrowings with deposit insurance premiums collected from thrifts. To the extent that this source was inadequate, the U.S. Department of the Treasury would kick in the rest.

The rationale for this circuitous financing mechanism was that it kept the $50 billion outlay off-budget. Only the Treasury's contribution to interest would appear on budget (plus financing required to cover old FSLIC obligations carried by the FSLIC resolution Fund). During debate on the bill, a strong push was made for direct Treasury financing on-budget. Such financing would be cheaper because Treasury bonds yield lower interest rates than REFCORP bonds would. The outlay could then be exempted from the Gramm-Rudman-Hollings deficit reduction targets for the same fiscal impact as off-budget financing.

FIRREA ultimately was passed with compromise funding. Thirty billion dollars came from the REFCORP funding plan. Another $1.2 billion came directly from the Federal Home Loan Banks. The remaining $18.8 billion came from the Treasury, on-budget. However, since the outlay from the Treasury came so late in the fiscal year, it did not affect the deficit reduction targets and necessitated neither an increase in taxes, nor offsetting expenditure cuts nor sequester.

The RTC requires not only money to cover the net losses that result from the insured deposits at a troubled thrift exceeding the institution's assets. It also requires up-front money, so-called "working capital." When an institution is resolved, an amount of money is spent initially in excess of the ultimate loss the Government will bear. This happens because the RTC retains some of (often most and sometimes all) the thrift's assets to sell at a later date. These outlays are therefore not permanent, but will be recovered later. The RTC is allowed to borrow to cover these up-front costs. Under a formula set out in FIRREA, RTC may effectively borrow up to 85% of the value of the assets it holds. These funds have been obtained from the Treasury's Federal Financing Bank. Because these borrowings will be recouped, they are also off-budget: were it otherwise, they would increase the deficit initially and trigger cuts in other domestic programs, only to produce offsetting income later as assets were sold.

PROGRESS AND CURRENT ISSUES

The process of dealing with troubled thrifts begins when an institution is placed into "conservatorship" with the RTC. It is open and continues to operate, but is controlled by the RTC as it awaits final resolution, going into "receivership." While in conservatorship, the institutions often shrink in size as the RTC lowers interest rates on deposits and funds flow out to other institutions. The process generates up-front expenditures by the RTC as it pays off withdrawn deposits. Because many institutions continue to lose money in conservatorship, RTC loss outlays consist not only of resolution costs but also of operating losses of institutions awaiting resolution. As of June 30, 1991, the RTC had taken control of 623 institutions, and was operating 193 of them.

Resolving Institutions

From August 1989 through June 1991, RTC resolved 430 institutions. Resolution takes three forms. First, an institution may be sold to a healthy institution (a "purchase and assumption" or P&A). Since the troubled thrift is insolvent, this procedure is effectively one of paying another institution to take it, with most of its assets intact. Second, an institution may be closed down with the depositors paid off directly and with the RTC retaining all the assets for sale later ("payout," or PO). Third, an institution may be closed down with the deposits instead transferred to another institution ("insured deposit transfer", or IDT). Again, the assets are retained for resale later. Since deposits are liabilities (i.e., the thrift owes the money to depositors), this last method requires the RTC to pay money to the institution acquiring the deposits; however, the value of the customer base is such that usually less than the face value of the deposits is paid. The RTC uses the resolution method that promises the least cost in each case. In POs and typically in IDTs, only insured depositors are paid off; uninsured depositors stand in line with other creditors to get a portion of their funds as assets are sold off. In P&As, uninsured depositors are effectively covered. On the whole, uninsured deposits in troubled thrifts are not large, since most uninsured depositors have removed their funds before the RTC has gained control of the institutions. In all cases, owners of the failed thrifts lose all their investment, and the old management is removed from power. Through the end of June 1991, 32% of resolutions were IDTs, 15% POs, and 53% P&As.

As of June 1991, 158 more institutions were ready to be placed into RTC hands. Another 300 or so were sufficiently troubled that they seemed likely candidates before the 1992 end date. The total may be even greater. Cost estimates for the entire post-FIRREA cleanup range from $130 billion to $175 billion in present value terms.

FUNDING

Even in 1989 when the debate over FIRREA was still going on, many analysts believed that $50 billion would be inadequate for the job. This has been borne out by events. By the end of FY1990, $32 billion had been spent in loss money. While still short of the $50 billion initially provided, this was beginning to constrain RTC operations from three different avenues. For one, because the RTC can only borrow up to 85% of its assets, loss money is immobilized in an amount sufficient to cover the 15% of assets which may not be borrowed. With $53 billion in working capital borrowed at the end of the fiscal year, $8.3 billion in loss funds were unavailable for resolution. In addition, funds must be kept to cover operating losses from conservatorships and administration costs that can be expected to occur until new funds are available. Finally, a reserve must be kept available in the event of deposit withdrawals from conservatorships, or when acquiring institutions exercise options to return assets that they have only provisionally accepted, inspected, and then rejected.

While $22 billion was provided to the FSLIC Resolution Fund to assist in renegotiating the 1988 deals and lowering costs, new funding for the RTC was held up in the waning hours of the 101st Congress. However, $18.8 billion in loss funding for the RTC was provided by utilizing an oversight in the FIRREA legislation.

The original legislation, as explained, permitted the RTC to borrow 85% of the value of assets it holds. More specifically, it said that RTC obligations could not exceed the sum of 85% of assets plus the unused portion of the $50 billion it was authorized to get from REFCORP. When the amount from REFCORP was lowered to $30 billion, no change was made in this section of the law. Consequently, with the approval of the Banking Committees, the RTC took advantage of this drafting error to borrow more funds.

By the beginning of March 1991, RTC activities were again constrained by lack of loss funds and $30 billion was requested by the Administration. (The RTC also expected to spend another $7 billion in working capital through the end of FY1991.) The outlays were to come directly from the Treasury without recourse to REFCORP. In accordance with 1990's budget agreement and the terms of the Omnibus Budget Reconciliation Act (OBRA), these outlays for the thrift cleanup would appear on-budget, but not count toward the pay-as-you-go requirements built into the deficit reduction targets. The $30 billion was appropriated in late March to cover the remainder of the fiscal year, but not before the RTC had to delay resolutions.

The cost of delay takes several forms. To prevent outflows of deposits from conservatorships that might drain cash, the RTC must pay higher interest rates on such deposits than it would otherwise. Further, it must slow the pace of resolutions and thereby incur greater operating costs. If the pace of the cleanup is slowed by reducing the number of institutions placed in RTC hands, it increases the losses that institutions then rack up before seizure. Finally, postponement of resolution may influence the bids received for failed institutions, and the way in which the sales are structured. The Administration estimated the costs of delay in March 1991 ran about $8 million per day.

The $30 billion, and $47 billion the RTC expected to spend in working capital, are to be used to reach total cumulative resolutions of 557 institutions before the end of FY1991. But the job of the RTC will still be far from over. More money for FY1992 will be needed then. Indeed, the administration has indicated that, depending on as-sumptions about how many more thrifts will fail, it will require at least $25 billion, and perhaps as much as $80 billion for the remainder of the resolution program. In all likelihood, the RTC's mandate will need to be extended further into the future in order to complete the job.

ASSET SALES AND RELATION ISSUES

After August 1992, as per FIRREA, the RTC will cease to take over insolvent thrifts (that task will belong to the FDIC) and will turn its' attention over to managing and liquidating assets, whether in conservatorships or received from resolutions. The growing magnitude of this task has already raised questions, however. The formal task is to dispose of assets quickly while gaining the greatest possible return for the Government, and having the smallest possible impact on market values for competing, privately owned, assets. In addition, there are strictures concerning necessary contracting for private services to handle the portfolio, and set-asides for certain assets. In real economic life, these ends are traded off against one other rather than attained simultaneously. In practice, therefore, the RTC must do a balancing act among the competing priorities.

The assets held by the RTC may be financial—cash, mortgages and other loans, securities—or they may be "real"—land, commercial properties, housing. As of the end of June 1991, the RTC had disposed of $172 billion but still held $160 billion in total assets. Of those held, $29 billion were in cash and securities, $70 billion were in performing loans, $26 billion were in delinquent loans, $21 billion were in real estate of all types, and the remainder were invested in thrift subsidiaries and other assets. Current estimates are that, by the time the RTC closes its' doors, it will have handled about $500 billion in assets.

Some assets are clearly easier to dispose of than others. Those being held in conservatorships, for example, still have a good percentage of cash, securities and "performing" loans and may be sold prior to receivership or along with deposits as a package to a purchasing institution (in a P&A). About 65% of asset sales throughout 1990 were from conservatorships. This proportion can be expected to decline, however, as more thrifts are resolved. By the time a thrift is in receivership, it is likely to have a much higher percentage of nonperforming loans and property taken in foreclosure, which are much harder to handle. At the end of calendar year 1990, for example 27% of conservatorship assets, but only 7% or receivership assets, were nonperforming loans and real estate. By the end of June 1991, the main difference in this picture was an increase in non-performing loans and real estate at receiverships to 39%.

A wide variety of problems, however, attend virtually all types of assets except cash and Government securities. Many securities, for example, are "junk" bonds which are currently saleable, even where they are not in default, except at very steep discounts. Discounts are also necessary for low-interest rate loans. Loans which are not current generally must be restructured to be disposed of, or must be foreclosed. Because it has been common practice for thrifts to deal in participations (sharing ownership of individual loans) the RTC may not have clear title to a delinquent loan and may not be able to restructure or foreclose unilaterally. This can be a severe impediment where a co-holding thrift which is not held by the RTC does not want to realize the attendant accounting losses on its books. Furthermore, where partial payments are being made on a loan, RTC moves to force restructuring may work at cross-purposes with regulator moves to encourage borrower to work-outs and ease "credit crunch" problems.

The problems of handling real assets are, of course, greater. Not only may title not be clear, but fire sale prices to move large numbers of properties quickly could seriously lower property values in nearby locations. Alternatively, holding to appraised values in weak markets guarantees long holding periods and carrying costs which can easily consume 2% to 3% of a property's value every month it remains unsold. Furthermore, for residential properties there is an additional mandate to give right of first refusal for certain properties to low-income housing providers and potential homeowners. The problem of selling quickly versus not undermining local property values is a complicated one. At least one early study indicates that the impact of RTC land and commercial properties sales is less than may have been feared. (See "The Impact of RTC Dispositions on Local Housing and Real Estate Markets," by Kerry Vandell and Timothy Riddiough, in Housing Policy Debate, Vol. 2 Issue 1, Washington D.C., Fanie Mae.) This is attributed to the fact that much commercial property is already occupied (rented) and does not constitute new space competing for tenants coming into a slow market. Further, market segmentation (appropriateness of space to specific types of uses or enterprises) effectively limits the competitive reach of such buildings. For raw land, location and legal uses have a similar segmenting effect. While these are plausible explanations for relatively little price-depressing effect from RTC marketing, another should also be kept in mind: the marketing of much of the commercial property, vacant or not, was anticipated and accounted for in prices already; i.e., the prices were already discounted in expectation of the increased supply for sale.

For residential sales, however, because vacancies are more common and market differentiation less, and because anticipation of sales may be less accurately reflected in prices, local property values may well be adversely affected by a temporary glut in units for sale. To the extent that values of houses are lowered by RTC marketing, increased mortgage defaults are probable and some amount of neighborhood instability could arise should values remain low for any length of time. The low-income housing set-aside (see below), under current procedures, has both pros and cons on this issue: under current procedures, the houses are reserved for 90 days for eligible buyers, following which, if they have not sold, they are conveyed at no price to qualified governmental and not-for-profit housing organizations. Prices of other houses could well be depressed by this procedure. On the other hand, the effects could well be offset in time by the very fact that markets are cleared of the overhand of unsold and unoccupied homes and apartments. Much depends upon how the succeeding owner-organizations handle the properties.

Nonetheless, the pressure is on the RTC to sell its assets quickly, mainly because of the funding problem, and the need to recapture funds for working capital. Because of the current restrictions on borrowing for working capital and the "hold" assets place on loss funding, some alternative ways of holding the RTC accountable for speedy sales without slowing down the closing of insolvent thrifts have been considered. Allowing 100% borrowing against held assets, but up to a preset ceiling amount, for example, would free the RTC from reserving loss funding to support assets, but (depending on the borrowing ceiling) could also retain the pressure to dispose of assets in a timely fashion. There are, or course, non-budgetary considerations: speedier asset disposition reduces carrying and maintenance costs, but rapid sales of the most liquid assets could also leave the RTC with marginal paper and property which could have been more successfully sold if bundled with the better assets.

Changes in procedure which reorganized market realities in many areas were announced by the RTC Mar. 25, 1992, and should speed asset sales. Among other changes, real estate which has not sold after 6 months may be marked down as much as 40% without a new appraisal (old procedures limited reductions to 20% after 9 months and required new appraisals before any further reduction). A new mortgage-backed securities program will be used to pool and sell mortgage assets, and collateralized bonds will be issued to sell the high yield ("junk") securities in RTC's portfolio. Also, RTC will provide seller-financing, where suitable commercial financing is not available, for a variety of property sales, aggregating up to $7 billion. For income-producing properties loans are limited to transactions with prices of not less than $500,000; terms may vary up to 7 years and down-payments should not be less than 15%. For residences, in general, terms must meet secondary market underwriting requirements.

AFFORDABLE HOUSING PROGRAM

FIRREA set out a program for diverting low-priced RTC housing into moderate-and low-income use. In general, housing units eligible for the program must be set aside for 90 days during which only moderate-income households seeking a personal residence or nonprofit agencies are eligible purchasers. All single-family houses priced no higher than $67,500 and multifamily units ranging in price from $28,023 to $58,392 (according to unit size) are eligible. Moderate-income families are those whose income is 115% or less of the area median income, and eligible nonprofits are those who agree to resell or rent to lower-income families whose income is 80% or less of area median. Where apartment units are rented, they must be affordable to tenants using approximately 30% of their income and at least 20% of units must be reserved for very low-income (50% of median) households.

The program got off to a very slow start with the first sales occurring in a small pilot program in the summer of 1990; buyers had to provide their own financing. Subsequently, the RTC attempted to put house sales together with set-asides from State mortgage revenue bonds.

Through calendar 1990, however, only about 2,700 single-family houses had been sold. No apartment buildings had been sold under the program, although some had been sold for market rentals out of conservatorships. Recent policy changes have made units still in conservatorships, as well as those held from receiverships, eligible for the program. The rental apartment side of the program still suffers from bureaucratic delays and appraisal problems; it remains to be seen if these can be resolved in a manner which allows several nonprofits—most notably, Volunteers of America, an affiliate of the Salvation Army—to use the program. Through May 1991, approximately 15,000 single family residences had been listed for sale under the program, and the RTC had accepted offers totaling $230 million on 7,100 such properties. The average sale price was $32,300 and the average income of purchasers was $22,100. In addition, $137 million of offers had been accepted for 90 multi-family projects comprising about 11,000 units. It has been estimated that as much as $20 billion or as many as 400,000 units could ultimately be eligible for the program.

Many of the difficulties of the housing program have involved financing problems, or the inability under the law of the RTC to cut prices much below initial appraisals. The latter problem was addressed by legislation and subsequent RTC actions in March 1990 allowing auctions with no minimum prices set for eligible bidders. And seller financing may be provided for both eligible families and nonprofits making bulk property buys. For families with incomes below 80% of the area median, interest rates will be set at market on 30-year fixed rate loans. Minimum downpayments are 3% for properties selling for $50,000 or less, and $750 plus 5% of the amount over $25,000 for higher prices houses. Where a purchasing family is the current renting tenant of the house, downpayments may be as low as 2 months rent, and interest rates may be discounted to as low as 7%. Nonprofits are expected to make equity investments of 5% and obtain first mortgage financing covering at least 60% of value in order to receive RTC-provided second mortgage loans.

ENVIRONMENTAL ISSUES

Among the properties over which the Resolution Trust Corporation has authority are lands that have significant environmental concerns, such as wetlands, floodplains, and coastal barriers. There are also properties that may have some form of environmental contamination that might give rise to liability for cleanup costs under some of the Federal environmental laws.

FIRREA nowhere details RTC's environmental responsibilities, thereby giving rise to considerable doubt as to the applicability of Federal environmental laws. There are, however, steps being taken by the RTC to ameliorate adverse environmental consequences of the disposition of properties. FIRREA required that the RTC inventory and publish, with twice-yearly updates, a list of properties with natural, cultural, recreational or scientific significance. The RTC will attempt to make sure that State and local government agencies having an interest in conservation as well as private conservation groups are notified as to available properties.

These efforts, however, may not be completely satisfactory to various groups interested in protecting the environment, and FIRREA may not give the RTC sufficient flexibility to arrive at creative solutions. If RTC's efforts fail, a legislative solution becomes more likely.

LEGISLATION

P.L. 102-18, S. 419

Resolution Trust Corporation Funding Act of 1991. Amends the Federal Home Loan Bank Act and Authorized an additional $30 billion to enable the RTC to meet its obligations to depositors and others by the least expensive means; requires several management reforms; allows sale of affordable housing without minimum purchase price; other adjustments. Signed into law Mar. 23, 1991.

H.R. 901 (Kostmayer)/S. 385 (Akaka)

Amends Section 21A of Federal Home Loan Bank Act to establish additional procedures and requirements relating to the identification and disposition of environmentally sensitive land and other property with natural, cultural, recreational or scientific values of special sig- nificance by the RTC. H.R. 901 introduced Feb. 6, 1992; referred to Committee on Banking, Finance and Urban Affairs. S. 385 introduced Feb. 6, 1992; referred to Committee on Banking.

S. 389 (Kerrey)

Amends the Federal Home Loan Bank Act to restructure the RTC Oversight Board and Board of Directors into a single governing entity. Introduced Feb. 7, 1991, referred to Committee on Banking.

FOR ADDITIONAL READING

U.S. Library of Congress. Congressional Research Service. *Banks and thrifts in transition*, by F. Jean Wells, et. al. [Washington] 1991. (Updated regularly) CRS Issue Brief 91003

FIRREA: *The Financial Institutions Reform, Recovery, and Enforcement Act of 1989*; a summary, by M. Maureen Murphy. [Washington] 1989.30 p. CRS Report 89-503 E

Housing finance restructuring: Changes and new issues created by FIRREA (P.L. 101-73), by William Jackson and Barbara L. Miles. [Washington] 1991. 19 p. CRS Report 90-522 E, 91-417E May 15, 1991

EVIDENCE 5

CRS REPORT FOR CONGRESS

Congressional Research The Library of Congress

Bank and Thrift Financial Problems, the Credit Crunch, and Lending to the Building Industry

Barbara L. Miles, Specialist in Housing and
William Jackson, Specialist in Money and Banking
Economics Division

SUMMARY

The commercial and residential building industries are experiencing losses, which some blame on lender reluctance to finance them. Such a visible aspect of the recessionary "credit crunch" is often attributed to collapses of thrift institutions and/or regulatory dislike of "speculative" lending to builders, in addition to the lack of demand for building activity. This report assesses these contentions.

BACKGROUND

In August 1989, The Financial Institutions Reform, Recovery, and Enforcement Act (FIRREA) was enacted to deal with the large numbers of failing and failed savings and loan associations ("thrifts"). The Resolution Trust Corporation (RTC) was brought into being to take over and liquidate these institutions. Through the end of calendar year 1990, RTC had taken over 531 institutions with assets of $270 billion. It may take another 500 thrifts before the cleanup is completed. Meanwhile, banks have experienced losses in their commercial real estate business, leading to many failures with the Federal Deposit Insurance Corporation (FDIC) taking them over.

Thrifts have traditionally been the most important lenders for housing finance, including major lenders to home builders for acquisition, development, and construction (ADC) purposes. The effect of thrift failures on builders is thus important. Unfortunately, analysis is necessarily tentative at this point and few hard data useful in for- mulating policy are available. Nonetheless, two tentative conclusions may be drawn. First, thrift failures per se have had relatively little effect on the building industry, although there are some clearly ad- verse exceptions. Second, changes in the regulatory environment stemming from FIRREA and new risk-based bank and thrift capital requirements have had effects ranging from temporary disruptions to apparent lending retrenchments - including in the commercial banking system.

FAILURES OF INDIVIDUAL THRIFTS

Changes due to failures of individual institutions affect builders who have outstanding loans or open lines of credit with the failed firms. When a thrift fails, RTC places it into conservatorhip. While in that status, the thrift is "downsized" - its assets sold off, or non-performing loans written down or renegotiated - in an attempt to get its losses under control and prepared for ultimate sale or liquidation. RTC may sell the thrift with some or all of its assets, the most common form of "resolution" of failed thrifts to date. In this case, a builder who has an outstanding loan or line of credit may find it conveyed to a new institution which has lending policies very different from those of the original; the builder may have to scramble to meet new terms or obtain fresh financing. This can be particularly disruptive where a construction project is underway and the builder is making regular draws against the committed financing to complete the project. In general, however, where performing loans are taken over by another financial institution, builders who are capitalized and/or profitable, or who have sufficient collateral to support lines of credit, are able to work through the disruptions with the new lender. Many builders had been able to turn to commercial banks for lending, at least until 1990.

The cases which have resulted in genuine "horror" stories appear to be those where the "new lender" is the Government regulator - in the case of failed thrifts, RTC. (The same stories have arisen when FDIC has been appointed the conservator for failed banks. FDIC essentially runs RTC as well). A builder's loans find their way into RTC's inventory of loans either because RTC paid off the failed thrift's depositors and took over all the assets directly, or because an acquiring institution refused or "put back" the loans to RTC along with other assets it did not want from a purchase. In such cases, a builder who may have counted on a rollover or refinancing could find loans called due instead, and outstanding credit lines canceled. There have been cases reported of builders whose loan draws were delayed without warning or explanation, forcing a slowdown in construction, which resulted in losses of sales. This then led to RTC reappraisals based on the lost sales, which led to reductions in the construction loan and a cash squeeze which forced builders to stop work altogether. Since the draws were needed to pay for work already done or materials already delivered, liens would be placed on the project by unpaid subcontractors and suppliers. This scenario which, according to the National Association of Home Builders (NAHB) has occurred at least a few times when Federal receivers have taken over thrifts and banks, may ultimately force projects and companies into bankruptcy and leave developments unfinished and sometimes decaying for lack of maintenance. Usually, such results are blamed on a combination of bureaucratic slowness in dealing with an industry where time is crucial, and ignorance of normal construction practices by conservators whose interests are in protecting the Government stake in bailing out depositors without regard to what may (or may not) prove to be increased losses. Situations such as this certainly have resulted in severe harm to some builders, yet their overall impact on the building industry is not clear.

CHANGE IN REGULATORY CLIMATE

The more important effects on builders may result from the change in regulatory climate since the passage of FIRREA and the need for all depository lenders to meet new capital standards. This change is only partly a reaction to thrift failures and international capital uniformity agreements. New appraisal standards (in FIRREA) and regulatory scrutiny of lenders' underwriting are also a reaction to prior sloppy and unacceptably risky underwriting by thrifts and banks whose sources of funds are Government-guaranteed. In particular, Comptroller of the Currency Clarke warned national banks about real estate lending in February 1990. His advisory to banks stressed deficiencies in their underwriting, appraisals, and documentation; and emphasized that examiners would take aggressive action on realty loans. the reaction reportedly was particularly severe in a critical region:

As real estate values throughout New England melted like snow in a premature thaw, a posse of OCC [Comptroller of the Currency] examiners descended on the region. Millions of dollars' worth of once-acceptable loans-such as the kind under which a developer can't rent all his space but is still making interest payments-were declared "non-performing," forcing the banks to post extra reserves. Like so many tumbling dominoes, cash-short banks cut their dividends, credit-rating agencies cut their ratings, and many bankers, figuring that Washington was telling them not to make so many loans, shut off the cash spigot that had helped fuel the region's growth.[1]

The resulting new credit underwriting standards (which were also applied by Federal Reserve and FDIC examiners) are probably the main reason for reports of the "credit crunch" phenomenon which apparently is making credit less available to many small businesses, especially builders. There is strong reason to believe that demands for credit are also lessened, due to the current recession, excess commercial capacity and office space, and the slowdown in the demand for housing. That final demands for what builders produce are slack is cause for lenders to be more careful in granting ADC loans than in the past, even for the most financially feasible projects and solid builders. Figure l (ed: figure not provided in 'Bailout') suggests the rise and fall of construction activity and one form of construction lending. The bank lending, however, is often less than overall construction contracts. (Both series are in nominal dollars, based to the year 1982.) Comparable thrift lending data are not available, but the downturn in their new construction lending is clearly greater. And lending by life insurance companies for income properties has experienced even wider swings up and then down.[2]

Stories of refused loans are now legion, and there is a case beyond lessened demand that good builders are having a tougher time getting financing. First, many builders borrowing large amounts for major projects have had to deal with FIRREA's limitations on loans to one borrower. A thrift may not lend an amount greater than 15 percent of its' capital to any one borrower. This rule has been in effect for commercial banks but was a reduction, from 100 percent or by a factor of six, for the thrifts. While the change has caused problems for builders with loans from overextended thrifts since enactment, it is a basic "safety and soundness" rule. One way builders can deal with the limitation is to work out

ADC loan participations in which several lenders, possibly including limited partners, put up the money with no lender breaching the 15 percent rule. Recently, the Federal National Mortgage Association received approval to set up such participations. The Association will make $50 million of its own money available for a demonstration program for housing construction; builders must match the funds.

Second, new capital requirements may be working against ADC loans. Lenders are required to hold capital equal to eight percent of assets, but the requirement is conditioned by the riskiness of asset categories. Home mortgages are in a 50 percent "basket" so that only four percent capital must be held. Commercial loans, including ADC, are in the 100 percent basket, requiring that a full eight percent be held. Should an ADC loan default, however, the lender could be forced to foreclose and take ownership of the collateral real estate. This is "real estate owned" and is in a 300 percent basket which requires capital equal to 24 percent. This configuration of risk baskets is very likely to result in stricter underwriting for builder loans than in the past, especially relative to other commercial loans. According to the NAHB, thrift and bank lending practices have tightened and lenders are requiring recourse loans (allowing the lender to attach personal or corporate assets beyond the project); greater documentation (to demonstrate creditworthiness of the builder and the project); greater builder equity or collateral (as the lenders cushion again default); and a variety of other changes. NAHB surveys of their member-builders also imply that the biggest changes may already be over: in the latter half of 1989, about 80 percent of their respondents reported stiffer requirements for ADC loans; in the fourth quarter of 1990, however, only 46 percent reported new tighter requirements with the rest showing no new changes. More recently, however, the National Association of Realtors surveyed 16,000 commercial real estate practitioners, finding that 95 percent had been adversely affected by limited availability of credit or restrictive terms of lending.

Third, builders seeking new loans or draws may be the marginal borrowers. This problem takes two forms. Where lenders must retrench, they are more likely to call in the good loans than the bad, simply because there is a higher probability of actually being paid. Bad loans, even if they must be written down, may only be recast because calling them could result in even greater losses. The second form occurs because lenders do not wish to increase any concentration of real estate loans. These loans, blamed by many observers for the thrift crisis, have become perceived as undesirable in themselves by such authorities as FDIC Chairman Seidman. He would have Congress give depository institution regulators the power to set standards on realty lending and reverse liberalized trends in 1974 and 1982 legislation.

RECENT DAMAGE CONTROL

On March 1, 1992, the banking and thrift regulators clarified a series of rules and guidelines, and proposed at least one change intended to make construction loans more available. According to the regulators, the new policies clarify that:

- supervisory examinations of real estate loans are based on the ability of the collateral to generate cash flow over time, not on immediate liquidation value;
- sound loans should continue to be made to creditworthy borrowers;
- problem loans should be worked out;
- and lenders may request review of supervisory findings.

Lenders are thus encouraged to work out loans which may be in temporary difficulty rather then simply end them; to make creditworthy loans without fear of supervisory policies; to challenge supervisory decisions which affect such loans adversely as a normal part of the regulatory process; and to continue reasonable loans to good customers despite having low or even below-minimum capital. Comptroller of the Currency Clarke has also recanted, in that his current view is that to fix rigid laws governing bank real estate activity would be inflexible and reduce management choices excessively.

These clarifications (and others) appear to constitute a signal not to overreact to the new capital standards (where the lender is on track to meet them) or to stories of overzealous examiners. In addition, where reappraisals of real estate in cyclically troubled markets could result in marking down the value of the loan secured by the real estate, it will be permissible to carry the loan at its cash flow assessment instead so that the lender will not have to write down capital and curtail new lending. This treatment is designed to prevent "fire-sale" valuation at far lower prices for the collateral than may be warranted. In addition, the March changes would allow examiners to "split" loans which are only being partially repaid. The practice has been to require such loans be placed entirely into "non-performing" status, disqualifying any partial payments from being treated as income and increasing loss reserves. With a split, the loan is divided into the amount supported by the partial payments (the performing part) and the balance which is in default. Builders may overcome temporary cash flow problems (as they often do) and return the full loan to performing status rather than declaring the full loan in default and accelerating its repayment. (It is uncertain whether the splitting rule will be adopted.)

Finally, much of the reported negative impact of the new lending environment may well prove to be temporary. To the extent that poor loans are not being made, and uneconomic projects not being funded, the economy and builders should be better off, so that the net effect may well be positive even if current standards turn out to be overly tight. Moreover, the boom in construction of the earlier 1980s - fueled in part by liberal tax laws and in part by economy-wide recovery from recession - produced a regional (Northeast, South) and national excess supply of apartments, offices, plants, retail space, and warehouses that may require years to fill up regardless of lending practices.

ADDITIONAL RESOURCES

Bankwatch Group Inc., Newsletter
The Atrium, Suite 4-A
457 Main Street
Danbury, CT 06811 - (203) 797-9999

Public Citizen's Congress Watch
215 Pennsylvania Avenue SE
Washington, DC 20003 - (202) 546-4996
The Botched Bailout: Restrucyturing the Resolution Trust Corporation. — ($20.00/copy)

Project Censored
America's CENSORED Newsletter
P.O. Box 310
Cotati, CA 94931
Available for $30 (USA) or $45 (Foreign)

Contact your local members of Congress for updates on the RTC and the recovery process. It's your Congress, your vote.

NOTES